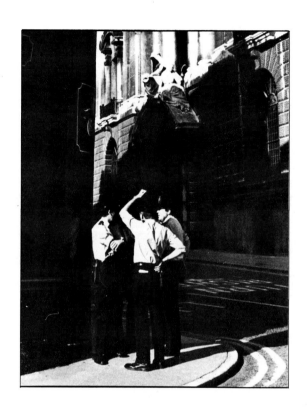

A Traveller's Guide to a

CELEBRATION
OF LONDON
Walks Around the Capital

Ian Norrie & Dorothy Bohm

A Traveller's Guide to a
CELEBRATION
OF LONDON
Walks Around the Capital

HTI

Historical Times INC.

Harrisburg

First published 1984 by André Deutsch Limited
105 Great Russell Street, London WC1

Published in the United States and Canada by Historical
Times, Incorporated by special arrangement with André Deutsch
Limited, 105 Great Russell Street, London WC1

A TRAVELLER'S GUIDE is a series title used courtesy of
Spectator Publications, London

Text copyright © 1984 by Ian Norrie
Photographs copyright © 1984 by Dorothy Bohm

Printed and bound in the United States of America by
Kingsport Press, Kingsport, Tennessee

First American Edition

Norrie, Ian
   A celebration of London.
   1. London (England)—Description—1981—
   I. Title   II. Bohm, Dorothy

914.21'04858   DA684.2

ISBN 0.233.97501.2

The photographs
are for Louis who always advised and helped,
and for our daughters, Monica and Yvonne
– Londoners by birth

The text is for Min,
who loves London,
and who accompanied me on the walks

Contents

Introduction

London is not one city, but two. Nor are the two neatly divided by a river, like Rome and the Vatican, or Buda and Pest; they are side by side on the north bank of the Thames. The smaller, older one, is called the City of London, the other is the City of Westminster.

'The City', as it is known, is a mere square mile on which the Roman citadel was founded, and is now the national centre of commerce and finance. It is theoretically, and often in practice, independent of Westminster which is the home of government and the monarch, and in which lie the Law Courts, the National Gallery and most of the theatres and major shopping streets of the capital.

Surrounding the two cities are the thirty-one boroughs of Greater London covering an area of nine hundred square miles. The walks in this book do not venture far into this urban sprawl, in which the majority of Londoners live, but do take the reader into parts of Camden, Lambeth, Southwark, Tower Hamlets and the Royal Borough of Kensington and Chelsea. On the whole they are confined to the City and Westminster.

Every Londoner knows what is meant by the City: few talk about Westminster, which is the name given to a cathedral, an abbey, a school, an underground station. Westminster has a city council, a city hall and a palace (better known as the Houses of Parliament). Perhaps actual residents (less than one quarter of a million) who pay their rates to the city hall think of themselves as belonging to Westminster, but it is more likely that they would say they live in Mayfair, Marylebone, Soho, Belgravia, Victoria — some of the components of an area which to a cockney, the generic name for a Londoner, are 'up West' — or in the West End which is what Westminster has come roughly to mean.

So when I write about the City I mean that square mile with a resident population of well under five thousand but a daytime workforce of perhaps half a million; when I refer to Westminster I shall often call it 'the West End'.

All cities are unique. Paris is better planned and less afflicted by modern architectural horrors; Rome, despite the Vittorio Emanuele monument, has developed more warily because of its antiquities; Istanbul is dirtier; Athens meaner; Madrid has more striking avenues (and traffic jams) and even more imposing banks; Copenhagen has more varied spires; Amsterdam has done better in preserving its commercial prowess without destroying its architectural heritage.

Lisbon, Prague and Buda, like Rome, are built on many hills; London, City and West End, is so comparatively flat that walking in it would be almost as undemanding as it is in Venice if it were not for the traffic. Such inclines as exist lead to relative pimples. St Paul's Cathedral is built on a trifling eminence to ascend which is as nothing set beside the effort required to climb the steps to its whispering gallery or, worse, those leading to the top of Sir Christopher Wren's Monument to the great fire of 1666.

And, as with any city, to walk it is the way to appreciate and understand London. The great Liberal statesman, William Ewart Gladstone, said it should be seen from the top of a bus. There is something to be said for this, but walking is less tedious. You can stop where you like, for as long as you like, unaffected by traffic congestion.

The eight walks described in this book cover, I believe, all the main, and some of the minor, sights of Central London, but I would not recommend that any itinerary be faithfully followed, paving stone by paving stone, canvas by canvas. For convenience I have included descriptions of particular galleries as they are encountered, but I would advise that the National Gallery, for instance, and the British Museum should not be made part of a day's walk. They should be the object of separate visits. This reminds me of a coach party at Stratford-upon-Avon. My wife and I were taking tea in an hotel there when a party of exhausted foreign tourists tottered in. Their courier, stifling yawns born of true fatigue, reminded her charges that they must be ready to take dinner before going to the theatre at 7.30. They could not decide whether to have tea and miss dinner, or vice versa. Many had both and then trailed off dutifully to a performance of *Two Gentlemen of Verona*.

Next morning, as we came down to breakfast, the poor souls were being shepherded into a coach to 'do' York, before setting out for Edinburgh.

That is no way to see any country or city. Walk it to appreciate the ambience, take pleasure in what is there, but do not risk cultural indigestion. Each of my walks ends in a green space; each involves many places of interest, but one person's stamina is less or more than another's, for all sorts of reasons. Do not feel beaten if you cannot complete the course. With luck there should be another day tomorrow, or a further visit next year. Always, I firmly believe, adopt the Links approach.

J. G. Links is the author of *Venice for Pleasure*, the best of all contemporary guidebooks. He is a learned man who imparts his immense knowledge without daunting the reader. His constant advocacy is along these lines: 'In that church over there is a painting by Tintoretto. It is an undoubted masterpiece but it will still be there tomorrow. So, if you are weary, sit at that delightful café by the canal, and enjoy a glass of wine or cup of coffee. Sit and soak up the atmosphere.'

London will still be here next year, nuclear holocausts allowing. Some of it will have changed for the better, some for the worse. In this book I try to describe how it appears to me in 1983. Much of it I love, some of it I detest but, even in Victoria, where architectural megalomania rules, there are still some appealing sights. The same is true of the City.

Two enduring features of London, its squares and its statuary, are mostly unimpaired by contemporary development, although both are marred by the ubiquitous pigeon and its droppings. Pedestrianization of streets is proceeding gradually, pavements are widened here and there, bus and taxi-only lanes are becoming more common, but vast hordes of citizens and visitors must be catered for. The shops need goods to sell, food and drink has to be delivered to pubs and restaurants – a city without traffic is unthinkable unless it has become as non-functional as Pompeii.

So London is noisy, bustling and, at the rush hour, harassing. Blue lights flash and sirens shriek as often as in other cities. Car horns blare when drivers become irritated (although not as fiercely as in Madrid), drop-outs plead in mutters or scream in abandon, but for most of the time people are going about their business or pleasure, and that is what I hope readers may do with this book, which is one man's celebration of London in words, and one woman's in photographs. We are both Londoners by adoption. So were William Caxton, Dr Johnson and Christopher Wren, to name but three of the illustrious many who have been drawn towards its twin cities. It has sometimes bothered me during my long term as a voluntary immigrant that many of those born, as were my children, within the sound of Bow Bells, care so little for the great city, or cities, in which they have grown up. I hope some one or more of them may be moved to wonder a little about London as a result of this book.

Walk One

Bank – Mansion House – Bank of England –
Royal Exchange – Guildhall – Museum of London –
Barbican – Smithfield – St Paul's – Fleet Street –
Dr Johnson's House – Staple Inn – Public Record Office –
Lincoln's Inn – Sir John Soane's Museum

*The City
from Waterloo Bridge*

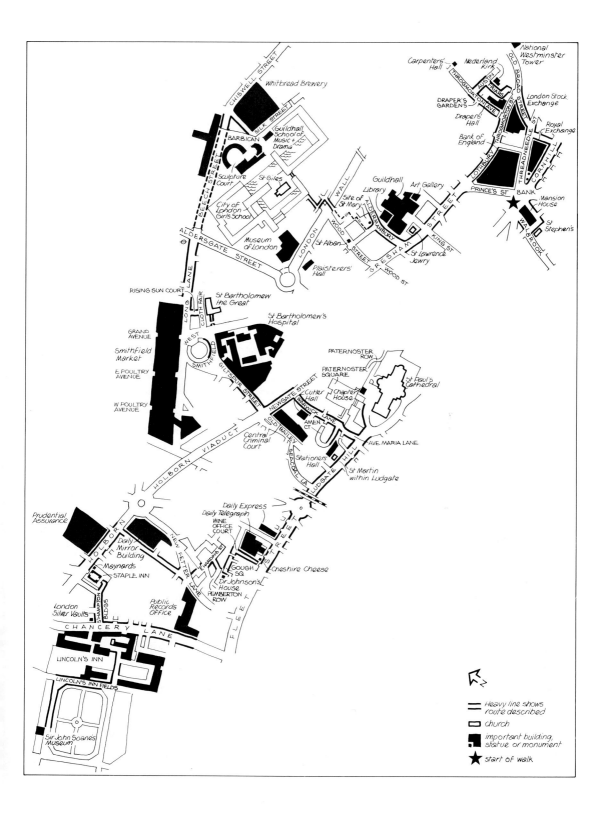

CHISWELL STREET

Whitbread Brewery

SILK STREET

BARBICAN

Guildhall
School of
Music +
Drama

Sculpture
Court

St Giles

City of
London
Girls School

Museum
of London

BEECH STREET

ALDERSGATE STREET

LONDON WALL

WALL

WOOD STREET

Site of
St Mary

St Alban

ALDERMANBURY

GRESHAM

R. WOOD ST

Plaisterers'
Hall

Guildhall
Library

Art Gallery

St Lawrence
Jewry

KING ST

PRINCE'S ST

Carpenters'
Hall

Nederland
Kirk

National
Westminster
Tower

THROGMORTON AVE

AUSTIN FRIARS

OLD BROAD STREET

Draper's
Gardens

London Stock
Exchange

Drapers'
Hall

Royal
Exchange

Bank of
England

THROGMORTON ST

THREADNEEDLE ST

CORNHILL

LOTHBURY

BANK

Mansion
House

St Stephen's

WALBROOK

RISING SUN COURT

LONG LANE

WEST SMITHFIELD

CLOTH FAIR

St Bartholomew
the Great

St Bartholomew's
Hospital

GRAND
AVENUE

Smithfield
Market

E. POULTRY
AVENUE

W. POULTRY
AVENUE

GILTSPUR STREET

SMITHFIELD

HOLBORN VIADUCT

NEWGATE STREET

WARWICK LANE

Cutler
Hall

Central
Criminal
Court

OLD BAILEY

AMEN
CT

Stationers'
Hall

SEACOAL LA

PATERNOSTER
ROW

PATERNOSTER
SQUARE

Chapter
House

St Paul's
Cathedral

AVE. MARIA LANE

LUDGATE HILL

St Martin
within Ludgate

Prudential
Assurance

HOLBORN

Daily
Mirror
Building

Maynards

STAPLE INN

NEW FETTER LANE

SHAMPTON BLDGS

Daily Express

Daily Telegraph

WINE
OFFICE
COURT

PEMBERTON ST

GOUGH
SQ

Dr Johnson's
House

PEMBERTON
ROW

Cheshire
Cheese

FLEET STREET

London
Silver Vaults

Public
Records
Office

CHANCERY LANE

LINCOLN'S INN

LINCOLN'S INN FIELDS

Sir John Soane's
Museum

N

═══ Heavy line shows
route described

▢ church

■ important building,
statue or monument

★ start of walk

Walk One   The first two walks start at what is known as Bank, the undoubted centre of the City, served by four underground train lines and several bus routes. The site was at the heart of Roman Londinium which thrived at a time when much of the territory described in the other six walks was uninhabited and, in places, swamp. Roman remains have been found, however, near Westminster Abbey on what was Thorney Island.

The Romans had arrived by AD 43. This is the first date in London's history, but it is probable that there were Bronze and Stone Age settlements although little trace of them has been found. Boudicca (Boadicea) sacked the first Roman town. As a consequence her Iceni tribe suffered such retribution that they must have been totally exterminated because there is no further record of them. The Romans rebuilt London, gave it walls, threw a bridge across the river and made it one of their largest cities in northern Europe. Its appearance is reconstructed in models in the Museum of London and elsewhere. There is little left of the Roman city, a few segments of wall, part of the temple of Mithras discovered under Walbrook in 1954, a small mosaic floor beneath All Hallows-by-the-Tower, a larger one found under Bucklersbury (now also in the Museum) and considerable numbers of smaller relics – coins, shards, household utensils. Archaeologists believe there is evidence of one of the supporting structures of the wooden Roman bridge below Upper Thames Street, and excavations are now taking place. Perhaps more will be revealed. An unlooked-for benefit of modern building methods, with their ability to drive deeper and deeper to find sure foundations, is what is revealed in the process. And such is the power of public opinion, that when some evidence of life centuries ago is uncovered, commerce has to bide its time while the archaeologists are let loose. The wartime blitz led to many discoveries of our past: so have the redevelopments of the last forty years. Suppose, just suppose, that St Paul's had to go – not a pleasant prospect – what might be found on Ludgate Hill, that site which was last the object of deep analysis after the fire of 1666? I would so much prefer my tax to be spent on underpinning Wren's marvellous cathedral, to find out what lies beneath, than on testing nuclear missiles. Ironically, the only way we may ever know is if anyone survives to forage amongst the ruins after a nuclear attack.

Because of the fire of 1666, and the pressure of commercial needs, which override almost everything in the City, there is not much of it visible today which pre-dates the 1850s. Most of it was developed in the nineteenth century, although based on the medieval street plans. For practical reasons, that could have been overruled, these were adhered to after the fire. Several opportunities were lost in

*The Bank of England
Lunchtime* (opposite)

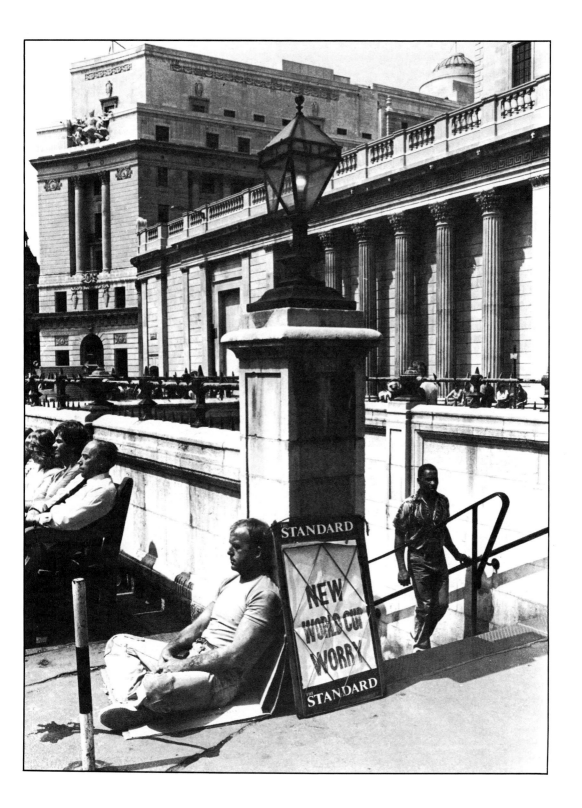

planning the city anew but at least the wooden structures favoured until the seventeenth century were replaced by others in brick and stone. It is a pity that the devastation of World War Two did not allow the St Paul's area to be redesigned so as to show the cathedral to the rest of London uncluttered by the mostly unglamorous approaches from which it still suffers. However, when we look at what has happened in other parts of the City we must be grateful that nothing more offensive has occurred.

There is a strong case for retaining the medieval street plan, and especially the street names, and, indeed, one of the charms the City possesses for visitors on a working day are the curious street signs – Crutched Friars, Fish Street Hill, Ship Tavern Passage, Puddle Dock, Poultry, Cheapside, Seething Lane, and so on. But there are no *roads*. The position of what were the gates in the Roman and medieval walls can be determined, at least approximately, by such names as Moorgate, Aldersgate, Newgate, etc.

The City measures one square mile. Some have called it a golden mile because of the riches which lie within it, or the fortunes to be made there. Dick Whittington, pantomime hero, but also four times Lord Mayor, and a real person, is supposed to have believed, as a poor country youth making his way on foot to the city, that its streets were paved with gold. So, in a sense, they were, for him and for many since. A square mile is a small area and, inevitably, these two walks which start within it will take us over the borders. When this happens we may not notice, but a city policeman would, as would a common councillor or alderman, or any of those who govern it.

On a weekday, from Monday to Friday, the City is all bustle, and because most of the pavements are narrow the visitor who stops, quite naturally, to stare, may find himself harassed. Yet in the evenings or on Saturdays and Sundays, when the streets are almost deserted and it is possible to dally in peace, it is *not* the City. Its personality has faded though it is undeniably more pleasant to explore.

On whatever day we start, it is at Bank, a meeting of six (some might say seven, even eight) thoroughfares around which are grouped the Bank of England, the Royal Exchange and the Mansion House. Let us observe the latter, the eighteenth-century mayoral residence, from the corner of Threadneedle and Princes Streets where two of the huge blank walls of the 'Old Lady', as the Bank is known, meet.

The Mansion House, Palladian in style, by George Dance the Elder, has a portico six columns wide standing on a stubby rusticated low ground storey with arched windows. There are steps up each side to the entrance and troughs of flowers between the columns. The pediment sculptures are symbolic of the City's opulence, with Plenty triumphing over Envy. The great rectangular house behind it overlaps the portico by two bays each side, and there are more pillars and a balustraded top floor. The interior, in which the Lord Mayor lives during his year of office, and where lavish receptions are held, is said to be magnificent but it is not open to casual visitors. On its west side is thin Walbrook, built over a stream which once flowed from the Wall into the Thames, and it was near here that the Roman temple of Mithras was uncovered when foundations were being dug for new office blocks. Thanks to the Legal and General Assurance Society the floor of it is preserved in front of the Sumitomo Bank building in Queen Victoria Street. It sounds ungrateful but to view it now, remembering the excitement of the discovery, is for me an anti-climax. There is little to see and it might well be more impressive in the Museum of London along with the artifacts found in it.

On this side of the Mansion House is an official notice board giving the names of the aldermen and councillors representing the ward – in this case, the Walbrook. (There are in all twenty-five wards.) Walk around behind the House along a passage between it and the church of St Stephen, a Wren masterpiece. Wherever we go in the City we shall come upon Wren spires and Wren interiors, many of them restored. The spires are all beautiful in their different ways, the interiors are all light and decorated with restraint. If I were to become responsive to the blandishments of religion it would have to be in one of Wren's churches which have nothing of the bleakness of nonconformist chapels, or of the gilt vulgarity so often evident in Roman Catholic places of worship. St Stephen's is being restored (yet again) but may be open by the time this is published. If so you will enter by steps beside the square tower which is surmounted by a steeple which goes up and up, stage upon stage, lantern upon lantern, ball upon ball upon ball until at last a cross tops everything else. Wren, although nearing the end of his long life, clearly enjoyed himself in seeing how far he could go. The church has a further surprise because the interior approximates to the Greek cross plan with a central dome, which Mervyn Blatch, in his *Guide to London's Churches*, suggests was the first ever in England.

In the north aisle of St Stephen's the architect and dramatist, Sir John Vanbrugh, is buried. His epitaph is:

> Lie heavy on him, Earth! for he
> Laid many heavy loads on thee!

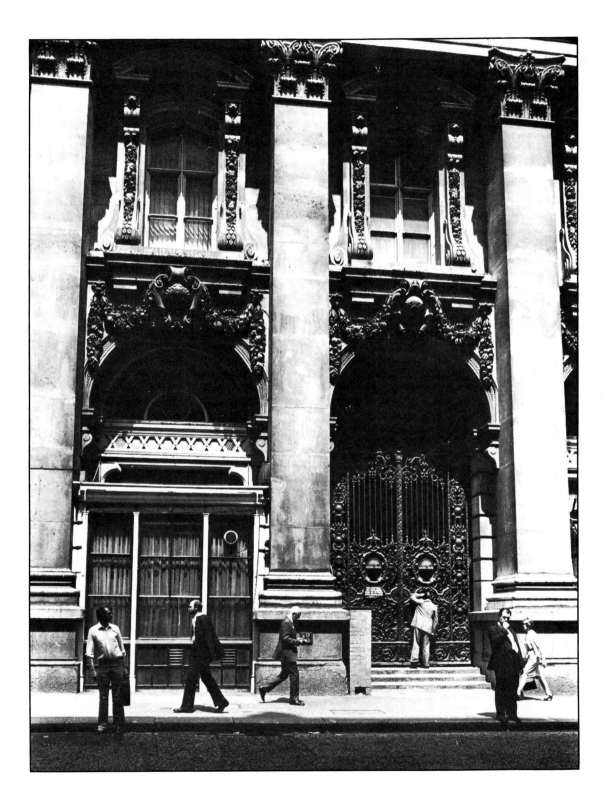

The Rector of St Stephen's founded, in 1953, the Samaritans, a nationwide group of voluntary helpers whose mission is 'to befriend the suicidal and despairing'. For this difficult and compassionate work many hope to be called but few are chosen, because just caring is not enough: Samaritans have also to be tough.

Return along the eastern wall of the Lord Mayor's handsome squat to look at the overpowering Bank of England lying within its protective outer wall, of which the late Colin MacInnes wrote that it was so neuter it was even fatiguing to walk around it. One of the two most scandalous architectural outrages committed between the wars was the almost complete destruction of Sir John Soane's eighteenth-century bank which was replaced by the present heavy edifice. (The tearing down of the Adelphi was the other. See Walk Five.) Yet this unwise demolition is now placed in perspective by the two gigantic horrors which arise behind the redesigned Old Lady of Threadneedle Street. They are the skyscrapers of the London Stock Exchange and of the National Westminster Bank, horrendous structures which, alas, are not alone in scarring the City's skyline. There is so much more, just as awful, to come that it is probably better to concentrate on what may be seen indoors or at eye level. The Royal Exchange, to which we lower our gaze, was conceived on a grand scale, on diminutive Cornhill.

Use a subway to reach it. There are many and they all lead out of a minor shopping centre around the escalators to and from Bank tube. There is a spacious courtyard in front of the Exchange which is no longer a bourse or place where merchants congregate. Sir Thomas Gresham built the first in 1566–8 to give the City a business centre worthy of a leading commercial capital. His building was burned in the Great Fire and its successor went up in flames in 1838, while its carillon of bells in the tower played the tune, 'There's nae luck about the house'. The present building survived the fire raid of December 1940 and is now mainly used as offices by the Royal Exchange Assurance Company, although there are shops in its outer walls. Until 1882 the inner quadrangle was unroofed but a severe winter with heavy snow led to its being covered over. After the Guildhall was blitzed its museum was moved here until it merged with the Museum of London which we visit shortly. Lloyd's, the shipping underwriters, had their premises in the Exchange close to the Coffee House where they originated, but moved to Lime Street before the Second World War. The Exchange is 300 feet long and 175 wide, the Corinthian columns at the main entrance rise 41 feet to support a pediment on which there is busy sculpture depicting commerce at its noblest. At the eastern end a baroque tower makes it appear that the exchange

The Royal Exchange (opposite)

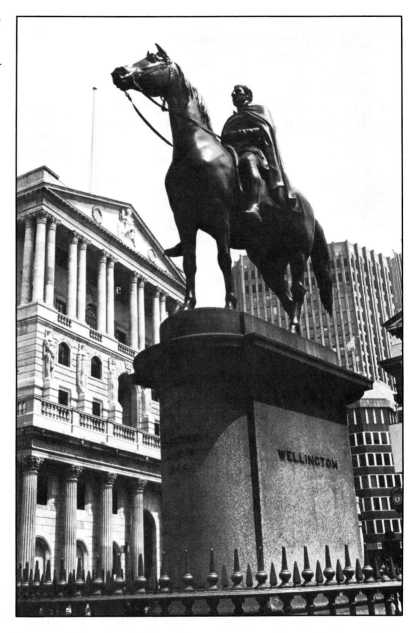

*Duke of Wellington
at Bank*

has engulfed a church, but it is just a tower from which, at three-hourly intervals through the day, traditional tunes chime out. The statue of the Duke of Wellington at the end of the courtyard was made from captured cannon. Between it and the frontage there is a war memorial which ought to have been sited more cleverly. At the other end, again, is a statue of the philanthropist George Peabody sitting upright, and rather tense, on a polished granite plinth. Near by is a stone bust of Paul Julius Reuter who founded his news agency at No. 1 Royal Exchange Buildings in 1851.

(Throughout this and the next chapter, especially, there are many references to both the Great Fire of 1666 and to that other disastrous conflagration of 30/31 December 1940, when incendiary bombs rained down upon buildings locked and unguarded because it was the weekend. For convenience I will refer to them hereafter by their dates alone.)

From the rear of the Exchange cross Threadneedle Street and, after turning to your right, bear left into Old Broad Street past the new Stock Exchange tower. There is a visitors' gallery here from which you can observe the brokers and jobbers and waiters broking and jobbing and waiting whilst the pound ails yet again and the City gets the jitters. Or you may be there on a bullish day when there are mad scrambles for the shares of a company for which there has been a takeover bid, and when the *Financial Times* index soars briefly. The jobbers are dealers in stocks and shares who buy and sell at one remove from the public, through brokers. The waiters, who wear gold-braided top hats and blue and red uniforms, are a reminder of the days when business was transacted in coffee houses. Their task is to carry messages between members who, apart from these colourfully dressed officials, are the only people permitted on the floor of the exchange. If a stranger contrives to get in, and is spotted, a member will start singing loudly and all the other jobbers and brokers will join in. It is at such moments that business may be seen, or heard, to retain some humanity.

The Stock Exchange stretches through to Throgmorton Street from which there is an arched opening into Austin Friars. Go under it and into a typical City street which quickly encompasses three right angles. At the last stands the Nederlander Kerk built in stone with a pretty little spire and weathercock. It is on the site of an earlier Dutch church which was bombed: an earlier one still replaced, in 1550, the Augustinian Monastery from which the street derives its name. It is open to visitors Monday–Thursday, 11–3, and also on Sundays for services. Turn left out of Austin Friars into Drapers Gardens and Throgmorton Avenue, a private road with no right of way whatever except for tenants and occupiers, so pretend you are visiting one or the other, and pass under cover to an open gateway. On the left is the back of the Drapers' Company building, then the Carpenters' Hall which, says Pevsner at his most succinct, is 'thickly Cinquecento'.

Dotted about the City in varying degrees of splendour are the halls of the livery companies. There are ninety-six companies which evolved from the Saxon frith-guilds for persons working in the same trade. Today they are more important for their role in the government of the City than in the organization of the actual craft they represent, although the Spectacle Makers still award diplomas to opticians, and the Goldsmiths' Company exercises control over those who trade in precious metals. The court and livery members of companies take part in the election of the Lord Mayor, Sheriffs and other officers of the Corporation but many members of most companies have little or nothing to do with the trade they represent. A merchant banker may be a Fishmonger, a white-collar trade union leader a Cooper, and so on. The companies are wealthy today not in most cases from actual trading but because of endowments and investments made long ago. Unless this is understood it may be a surprise that the Fanmakers, in this day and age, should have a handsome hall. The Farmers did not have a livery company until 1952 and Accountants only achieved this status in 1977, which is mysterious because accounting has been a prominent City occupation for a long while, but I wonder when the land was last farmed? The City is proud of its companies and halls, many of which have been rebuilt or restored since the Second World War. It is important to realize this because there is no institution more conscious than the City of preserving its ancient traditions and at the same time exploiting every possible commercial advantage. The annual Lord Mayor's Show, a splendid pageant with colourful floats and costumes, held every November, is a good example. The gilded coach rumbles along City streets between new high-rise buildings which demonstrate a ruthless determination to celebrate the profit motive.

Throgmorton Avenue leads us back into the street of the same name which becomes Lothbury as the Bank of England looms into view again on your left. A statue of Soane in a niche in the wall relieves the monotony somewhat; yet another branch of the NatWest, facing it, does not. Cross Moorgate into Gresham Street where, at the junction with King Street, is the church of St Lawrence Jewry, the Guild Church of the Corporation of London. The name Jewry may seem in questionable taste since this was the area of the City in which the Jews lived until they were expelled in 1290 by Edward I. Several of the city companies hold their annual services here, including the Girdlers who have done so since 1180. It is on an ancient hallowed site, and was rebuilt by Wren after 1666; it was gutted in 1940 and restored with a fibreglass spire in 1957. It is a spacious, light church standing obliquely to Guildhall, the home of City government since early medieval times. The present hall is basically of the fifteenth century but it has been so subjected to fire, bombs, planners and restorers that something of each of the last six centuries can be seen.

The roof had to be replaced in 1940, as had the huge wooden figures depicting Gog and Magog. Probably legendary creatures, to whom there is a Biblical reference, their London connection is that they were descended from the murderous daughters of the Roman emperor Diocletian, and became porters at the Guildhall. This does not explain why they are so revered in City history, but they have been carved anew and stand in the hall where the Lord Mayor's Banquet is held each autumn. This, by tradition, is attended by the Prime Minister who usually makes it an opportunity for pertinent political comment, or even to confirm policies which may not be popular in the City. In the past trials for treason have taken place here; nowadays it, and the ancient Undercroft, a spacious light crypt, are more likely to be used for receptions and parties. Attached is the Guildhall Art Gallery and Library, the former now used only for occasional exhibitions. The Guildhall School of Music and Drama, founded in 1880, is now in the Barbican.

*Wine bar
at the Royal Exchange*

The frontage of the Guildhall is a hotchpotch of classical and Gothic with some Indian thrown in. It doesn't offend because the fifteenth-century dimensions still rule, the roof is nicely pinnacled, and there is much variety around the Yard: a gracious early nineteenth-century house (Irish Chambers) and a newly erected block with a curious, almost detached, gatehouse on four concrete legs. The latter also has a small spire above a sloping roof with meurtrières in it (perhaps for the use of the Archers, although they don't have a company). The City coat of arms is on the front. It is a not unpleasing complex and illustrates the ever-developing City.

What is immediately to come could be termed the Developed. Apart from a few small stretches of Roman wall, the restored tower of St Alban, Wood Street, and the Church of St Giles-without-Cripplegate, which is incorporated into the Barbican, almost everything else on both sides of the dual carriageway called London Wall is new, mostly garish and almost always overpowering. Gigantic upended rectangles of glass straddle the scene and ruin the skyline. Near the bases of some of them are catwalks to take you across the main road and into the Museum of London and the Barbican. Before joining one of them dally a while in Aldermanbury, into which you have turned right from Gresham Street, where a garden has been made on the site of St Mary's church. A bust of Shakespeare stands here which once stood outside the church where John Heminge and James Condell were buried. Blessed men, those two printers, but for whom there would be none of the bard's plays to perform. Having paid homage, make across London Wall and turn left to the Museum which lies beneath an especially monstrous block in turgidly coloured glass called Bastion House. Beside it is a preserved section of the ancient wall in the trim grass, next to a Queen-Anne-type building, surely bogus because the area was entirely flattened, but pleasant to behold anyway. Across the way by the quaintly named but contemporary Plaisterers' Hall is another relic of wall.

The Museum of London was officially opened in 1976 by the Queen. It is an amalgamation of the City's Guildhall Museum, founded in 1826, and the first London Museum which was in Lancaster House from 1912 to 1945 and, thereafter, in Kensington Palace. The permanent exhibits are laid out around a well on two floors connected by a glazed ramp. It relates the story of London chronologically, from the Thames in Prehistory to the twentieth century, with an added section on ceremonial which has as its centrepiece the Lord Mayor's state coach, made in 1757, and still in use.

For a reason which is obscure to me the excellent spiral-backed guide with a leaf for each historical section starts with Ceremonial London and works backwards to Prehistory in precisely the opposite way to the natural route around the museum.

In the Prehistory section there is a flint hand axe said to be about 200,000 years old, a pottery bowl found at Heathrow when the airport was being constructed in 1944, a model of what the village there may have looked like about 600 BC, and, of course, much else.

The Roman section has the mosaic floor found in Bucklersbury in 1869, and marble heads unearthed in the Temple of Mithras.

In the sections which follow are Saxon brooches, a Viking grave slab, a reconstruction of Old St Paul's, a fifteenth-century carved doorframe from St Ethelburga-within-Bishopsgate, embroidered Tudor costumes, and a highly coloured Delft plate honouring Elizabeth I.

In the Early Stuart and Commonwealth section there is an audio-visual presentation of the Great Fire, and Cromwell's deathmask, while down the ramp in Late Stuart you will find Samuel Pepys's chess set, a sedan chair and period furniture. Next, in Georgian, there is David Garrick's dressing-table from Drury Lane Theatre and a reconstruction of a cell from Newgate Prison. The exhibits get larger as the centuries roll by. In the Nineteenth-Century Hall there is a fire engine, a Board schoolroom and a Victorian kitchen. Shop interiors feature in Imperial London along with a public-house bar. The Twentieth Century exhibits include models of cars, suffragette posters, collections of cigarette cards and a broadcasting studio.

There is provision for push- and wheel-chairs, a shop selling books, slides, cards etc., and also an area for temporary exhibitions. The Museum is closed on Mondays even in the school holidays. This is tiresome because children are much attracted to it. The very layout appeals to them. For adult visitors, and for them, it is the best of introductions to London's history.

Return along the catwalk by which you came, past the large metal scroll with a quotation from John Wesley adorning it. (This concerns the revelation he had in a chapel in Aldersgate Street – now hidden by this development – which led him to stomp around the country terrifying the simple-minded by his bleak message.)

Follow signs to the Barbican Centre, and with luck, you may reach it. Since it opened in the spring of 1982 Londoners have enjoyed swapping stories about the difficulties of getting into, through and out of the Centre, of failing to discover the entrance to the car-parks, or the location of the exhibition halls, or of becoming lost in residential quarters. Some of what is recounted is exaggerated, but not all, because the designers do seem to have displayed a talent to confuse.

First, however, I should explain what the Barbican Centre is and how it came about. It is in the old Cripplegate Ward of the City, just beyond the walls, around an area where there was once a watchtower-cum-gateway, or Barbican. Some seventy acres, much of it the centre of the rag trade, was laid waste in 1940. It lay in ruins for the remainder of the war, and for long after, whilst various schemes for its rehabilitation were proposed and considered. Eventually the government suggested to the Lord Mayor that a new residential estate should be created, and this was agreed in 1959. As a result three towerblocks of flats, each over thirty storeys high, were erected, along with a number of lower ones. Building commenced in 1962 and the first units were ready to be lived in six years later. Meanwhile recommendations had been heard for creating an arts centre which would provide a permanent home for the London Symphony Orchestra, the Royal Shakespeare Company and the Guildhall School of Music and Drama. It was also to incorporate an art gallery, sculpture court, library, three cinemas, exhibition halls, restaurants, bars and waterside café, and a lake with fountains. The Court of Common Council approved the scheme in 1971.

It is unfortunate that the first proposals came when skyscrapers for residential accommodation were still in fashion but even without them the Barbican complex would be Orwellian, and it is shivery to think that the completion date was so close to 1984 – always supposing it has been completed. Yet the Centre has good points. It is spacious and informal and provides in this crowded city an extra place where people may sit in the open air away from the traffic fumes and noise, although on a windy day the fountains can drench those using the Waterside Café. It is also good that St Giles was restored and made part of the scheme although it does look anachronistic. This is emphasized by the proximity of the new City of London School for Girls. And it may be that when the Sculpture Court acquires some sculpture the arid empty space within the crescent of conference rooms and offices will become more endearing. Not at all so is the barracks-like atmosphere of the various residential blocks, which have between them over two thousand flats, nor is the road tunnel between some of them and the exhibition halls. Nor the sign reading DISABLED LAVATORIES (if they are permanently so, something should be done about them).

The Barbican concert hall seats 2,026, and the theatre, on two levels with open stage, 1,166. The theatre does not have dividing aisles, which is unpleasant for those with claustrophobic tendencies, and inexplicable in view of the London Fire Services' concern for our safety.

The Centre, and its surrounds, is certainly an improvement on the devastated site of the 1940s and 1950s but it lacks the homeliness and variety, the tattiness and humanity, of the quarter which was blasted away. Each visit to it makes me more rather than less critical. A park over the seventy acres on which it is built, with a smaller centre to provide some of the amenities, together with a few houses and gardens would have been a greater improvement.

Inevitably it has to be compared with the older South Bank complex which we shall visit on Walk Five. Visually neither excites me as a whole, but the Royal Festival Hall is surely superior to any other building on either site, and the South Bank also has the advantage of being beside the river.

Leave the Barbican by the exit to Silk Street, if you can find it. If you cannot the rest of this walk is in a shambles!

Turn left and walk a few yards towards Chiswell Street where you will see ordinary-sized old-fashioned buildings which escaped the blitz. On a corner, as you turn right into it, is a wine bar where, in the

Smithfield Market

vaults, is a restaurant, favoured by those who have escaped from the Barbican exhibition halls. (Reservations essential for lunch.) Also in Chiswell Street, where it has been since 1749, is Whitbread's Brewery. Most of the present building is later but the Porter Tun Room, which at the time of writing still houses the Overlord Embroidery, dates back to 1774. The tapestry, mainly depicting the Normandy landings of 1944, has drawn insufficient crowds and is to be removed to a new site in Portsmouth. I hope this imaginative work will fare better there.

So, having admired the softly coloured brickwork of the brewery, and a pleasant terrace opposite, retrace your steps into Beech Street, and enter the gloomy road tunnel ending at Aldersgate Street opposite the Barbican tube station. Cross into Long Lane which leads to Smithfield Market, a solid, workmanlike structure with domes on towers at every corner. There has been a market here since about 1200. The interior is divided into six by Grand Avenue, and East and West Poultry, wherein hang raw carcases and unplucked birds. A turning off is Rising Sun Court which leads into Cloth Fair. Along most of one side of it is the priory church of St Bartholomew-the-Great. It, and the nearby hospital, 'Barts', were founded early in the twelfth century by the monk Rahere, who, on recovering from malaria, forsook life as a courtier and devoted his remaining years to good works. Little is left of his church but sufficient to show from the massive simple rough columns and arches at the west end of the chancel what a splendid Norman building was here. The nave was demolished after the Dissolution, so we look towards the altar down the chancel, on the south side of which is a happy conceit: an oriel window with stone mullions built so that a prior – lame perhaps, or lazy – could attend mass without leaving his cell. Above is the clear window of the apse, originally the end of the building, beyond a lady chapel built in the fourteenth century. This, like the rest of the church, had a chequered career, becoming a printing shop (Benjamin Franklin worked there) bordered by a factory. Elsewhere there was a school and blacksmith's forge, and the cloisters were used as stables. St Bartholomew's escaped both major fires but was ravaged by neglect in the centuries between them. In the nineteenth century Sir Aston Webb restored it with great feeling for its heritage; in the twentieth part of one cloister was reopened. The gatehouse through which we go into West Smithfield is of the thirteenth century although its timbers have been much renewed. It does, however, give a fleeting impression of how medieval London looked.

St Bartholomew's Hospital, which comes next, resembles a college with its courtyards and closes. It is largely eighteenth-century but has

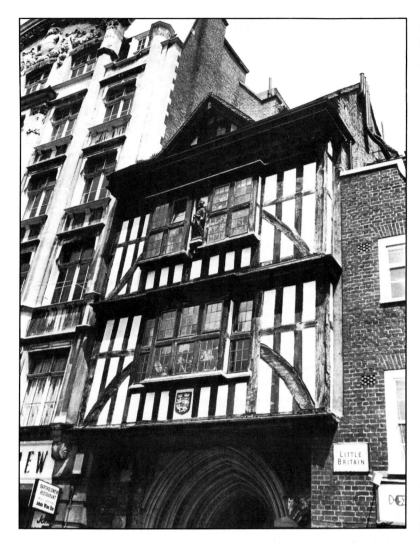

also been much altered: nothing of its Norman origins can be seen,
which may be a comforting thought for patients.

Go down Giltspur Street to the crossroads with Holborn Viaduct,
Newgate Street and Old Bailey. Newgate Prison once stood here:
outside it the last public execution took place in 1868. On the corner
of the Old Bailey is the Central Criminal Court, which requires no
further explanation. Turn left, then, into Newgate Street, opposite a
large, dirty, anonymous building on which there is a plaque to tell you
that this is the site of Greyfriars Monastery (does this bring to mind
thoughts of pious monks or of Billy Bunter?) and cross into Warwick
Lane. On your right is Cutlers' Hall, with a frieze of artisans labouring

away at stonework, and, when Warwick turns into Ave Maria Lane, there is another livery hall, that of the Stationers. The roof was burned when the publishing centre around Paternoster Row was laid waste in 1940, but the treasures within survived. Apart from official functions of the Stationers' mystery, it is now the setting, annually, for the Booker-McConnell prize dinner at which one fortunate novelist receives a cheque for £10,000. I was once there when the most eminent bookseller of this century was made an honorary freeman of the company. After some heraldic business from the Master and his acolytes, the Clerk called out 'Fetch Sir Basil Blackwell from the Stockroom' and, with all the dignity which that gentleman might have mustered to carry a valued volume from his own stockroom in Oxford, a procession of liveried persons emerged to come before the Master for the ceremony: it was a moving occasion.

Next to the hall, through a narrow passage, is Amen Court, a delightful eighteenth-century backwater, where some of the clergy of St Paul's dwell. Opposite is a car-park and staircase leading up to Paternoster Square, as it is laughingly called. There has been no attempt at restoration here. Nothing remains of its pre-war character and I would avoid its aridity, especially if you feel any nostalgia for what was for centuries the centre of the book trade. Walk instead to the end of Warwick Lane and turn left to experience your first full view of Wren's cathedral, to visit which is the highlight of this particular walk.

Most English cathedrals are in the Gothic style. This one is not because of 1666. Mercifully it is not in the modern idiom either because it escaped 1940, with bruises only, which is astonishing because Hitler's bombers were said to be under instructions to destroy it. It was then the largest single building in the City and easily identifiable, I imagine, from the air. It was indeed struck by one bomb which demolished the altar, and by two more which failed to explode; also by many incendiaries which bands of fire watchers extinguished before much damage was done.

The earlier conflagration was really a blessing, and not only for St Paul's. It enabled Christopher Wren to exercise his genius for designing buildings both secular and ecclesiastical, although, in the City, it was mostly the latter. Eighty-four City churches were burned out in 1666; forty-nine were rebuilt or replaced and Wren had a hand in all of them. His involvement after the initial stages was, in some cases, peripheral, but he was with St Paul's every step of the way, even into extreme old age. Before the fire, when he had already started to turn his attention from astronomy, anatomy and mathematics to architecture, he had been involved in surveying Old St Paul's. This

The Old Bailey
(opposite)

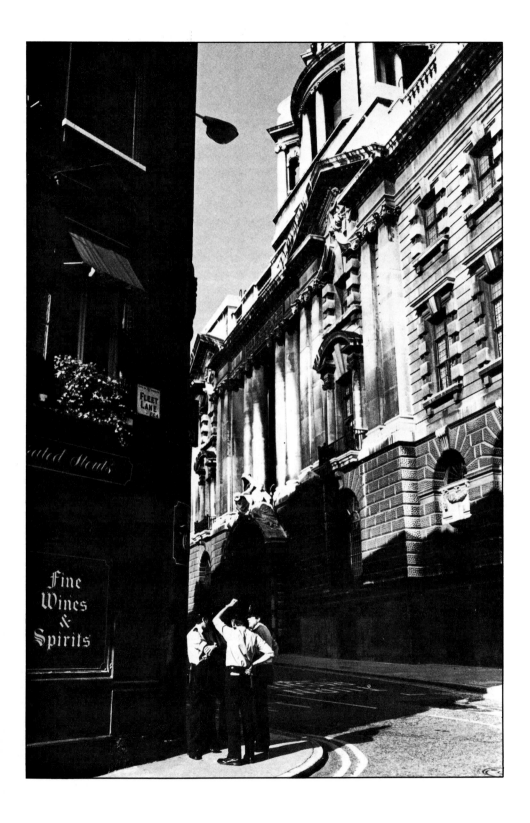

was after Inigo Jones's partial restoration of 1634–43. Jones had found the Norman cathedral built between 1087 and 1240 in a grossly neglected condition.

Wren's wrangles with the cathedral authorities and with Parliament about the rebuilding have been told in many books. He submitted three plans. The model for the second of the two rejected

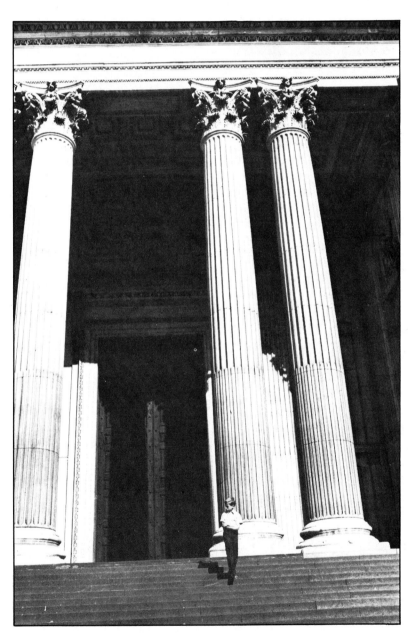

St Paul's Cathedral

may be seen in the crypt, but the third, known as the Warrant Design, needs no model. It was called 'Warrant' because its acceptance had a let-out clause for the architect to make 'variations, rather ornamental than essential'. Wren chose to interpret this in the widest sense and the result is, roughly, what we see today. The foundation stone was laid in 1675, in 1708 the architect's son placed the last stone on the very top of the lantern. In 1710 the dome was finished. That so massive and fine a building should have taken only thirty-five years to be completed is amazing; that members of Parliament became impatient with Wren's progress and withheld his salary for many years was outrageous. At the moment of completion Wren was 78 and his classical approach to architecture had given way to Baroque. He was not only old but out of fashion.

St Paul's is a marvellous building by any standards. Its superb dome has a diameter of 112 feet and rises, with cupola, lantern and cross to 365 feet above ground level. The cathedral is 515 feet long and 248 wide at the crossing. In fact there are two domes, Wren having built an inner one which, with the brickwork over it, supports the outer one and the lantern. It was a triumph of innovation which was excellently illustrated in a television film some years ago.

St Paul's ranks as the number one sight in London. Royal marriages take place here, the funerals of the great start from here, it is the scene of national thanksgiving services. The inside is magnificent but not ornate. There are indeed many decorations and ornaments but the sheer size of the interior tones them down. I am not certain that I would include the High Altar and Baldacchino in this comment but if you recall Bernini's monstrous contribution to St Peter's, this looks modest and tasteful.

You may inspect the inner dome at closer quarters if you have a good head for heights and feel inclined to climb hundreds of steps to the Whispering Gallery. It is so called because if you stand at the entrance you can hear what is being said in a normal voice across 107 feet.

In the south-west corner of the cathedral is a geometrical staircase of much beauty made by William Kempster, a master mason employed by Wren. The only surviving decoration from the pre-1666 building is a white marble effigy of the poet John Donne who was Dean from 1621 to 1631. He posed, dressed in a shroud, for a painting from which the statue was modelled.

To visit the crypt where many famous people including Nelson, Wellington and Wren himself are entombed, there is a small charge collected by a courteous and smiling official. Nelson's tomb was originally intended for Cardinal Wolsey, but he fell from favour. Then

Henry VIII had his eye on it for himself and Anne Boleyn, but after her execution it lay neglected at Windsor for nearly three hundred years. At least it is simpler than Napoleon's. Also in the crypt is the OBE chapel for members of that Order of the British Empire, created in 1917 just in the nick of time, you might say. As hundreds of new members are created in every honours list one must hope they don't all come to worship simultaneously. (There is also a chapel for the Order of St Michael and St George, which has fewer members – no doubt that is why it is larger – which lies to the right of the main entrance; behind the altar is the American Memorial Chapel.)

The choir at St Paul's sings in the Quire, a word now more usually associated with paper-making, but every great institution must be allowed its idiosyncrasies. This is no mean Quire, adorned as it is with the exquisite wood carvings of Grinling Gibbons who was recommended to Wren by John Evelyn, the diarist. Another fine embellishment is Jean Tijou's wrought-iron gates to the north and south of the chancel. They are copies of the originals which stood in Old St Paul's.

St Paul's is not rich in paintings although much attention has been paid to Holman Hunt's *The Light of the World*, reproductions of which are popular with visitors. Hunt, who was a founder member of the Pre-Raphaelites, is buried in the crypt.

Before or after your visit walk around the outside of the cathedral noting, to the north of the churchyard, the handsome Chapter House, and St Paul's Open Space, the name given to the old burial area plus an additional patch of ground added to it when a road was closed in 1966. To the east the tower of an anonymous Wren church has survived, attached to a modern building which is the new Choir (not Quire) School. There are many seats and trees. The railings around the churchyard were cast at Lamberhurst, Kent, in 1714.

As I write, the exterior of St Paul's is being cleaned and it is looking positively dazzling. There are Super Guided Tours of the cathedral at 11.00 a.m. and 2 p.m. on all weekdays. Photography in the interior is, unfortunately, permitted. The steps outside are a favourite place for rendezvous and many a tired tourist sinks on to them, as perhaps you will, before setting off on the final lap of this walk which leads down Ludgate Hill. On the right is the small church of St Martin-within-Ludgate, the spire of which was intended by Wren as a foil to the great dome of his cathedral. The records do not go back before the twelfth century but a wall plaque claims that there was a church here in the seventh, built by King Cadwallader, about whose feats the reader may well be hazy. As in many City churches lunchtime organ recitals are given in the peaceful interior.

On your way to Ludgate Circus you pass on your right Seacoal Lane, a reminder of the days when coal barges unloaded their cargoes beside the River Fleet which flowed into the Thames at Blackfriars. It was completely paved over long ago but can still cause damp, and even flooding, problems for those who live on its course. It was navigable for several miles, and is remembered locally in the name of Fleet Street, which lies across the Circus, and is still thought of as the headquarters of English journalism, although the newspaper industry has spread to other parts. Monuments to its prosperous but not always glorious past are still here and in use, the most prominent being a horror in mostly opaque glass erected in 1932 and dedicated to Beaverbrook's Express Group. It has been described in *Private Eye* as 'Black Lubyanka'. The *Daily Telegraph* building further along is less offensive. Turn right into Wine Office Court, past Ye Olde Cheshire Cheese, a famous inn rebuilt in 1667, and follow signs to Dr Johnson's House which is our next stopping-place. It lies at the end of Gough Square, a small oblong paved area. Samuel Johnson compiled the first English dictionary and was further immortalized by James Boswell in the famous *Life*. The irascible doctor lived here from 1748 to 1759 so as to be near William Strahan, the printer of his lexicon. In the attic long tables were laid out for his work. There are seven rooms to visit on four floors and in each there are guides shaped like butter pats, indicating the various pictures, books, ornaments, furniture to be seen. The floorboards creak, and you may well be the only visitor, but the custodian will leave you alone or be ready to assist if you ask for more information. On the ground floor is a precious copy of the first edition of the *Dictionary*. It is open so that you may examine some entries but you are forbidden to touch it. Cecil Harmsworth purchased the house in 1911 when, he wrote, 'it presented every appearance of squalor and decay'. Thanks to him it was turned into a museum which he was determined should not be fusty, so he resisted many offers of Johnsoniana, to prevent the house becoming cluttered. It suffered grievously in the Second World War on three occasions but has been successfully restored.

When he moved in 1759, Johnson went to live in Staple Inn to which we too now repair by a slightly tortuous route to the north, taking us first into Pemberton Row, then East Harding Street, where we cross into the courtyard of Newspaper House. Here is a much stained concrete sculpture of three men – newspaper workers, I suppose. One of them is very correctly dressed and looking supercilious, head held high, ignoring the open book on his lap. Leave by steps opposite which bring you out, under another building, into New Fetter Lane. Cross to Fetter Lane which leads to Holborn, joining it opposite the Prudential Assurance Building, a symbol of respectability and stolid wealth in red brick Victorian Gothic. Gamage's store has gone, replaced by a new monster which is not as high, however, as the *Daily Mirror* building. That dwarfs everything around here and is as neuter as the screen wall of the Bank of England. Ignore it and, when you reach Maynard's sweet shop, look up and study the only preserved Tudor houses in London. They date from 1557 and have three overhanging storeys. The Old Houses, as they are known, were reconstructed inside in 1937 but the outside is authentic, always allowing for the necessary maintenance over the centuries. Beneath them is a passage into Staple Inn which was almost entirely destroyed in the blitz but has been carefully reconstructed with attention to the finest detail, and with such original materials as could be salvaged. The courtyard is square with a paved and cobbled surface and a large round seat. There is a traditional lamp-post with

*Inns of Court
(Middle Temple)*

an arm from which dangles a metal flower bowl. By the Porter's lodge is a notice which reads:

> The Porter has orders to prevent Old Clothes Men & Others from calling articles for sale. Also rude children playing & C. No horses allowed within this Inn.

Samuel Johnson lived at No. 2 during 1759 and 1760. Staple Inn was founded as one of the Inns of Chancery (see below) in 1545, and first rebuilt in the eighteenth century. Leave it by a passage through a garden which winds to a gate leading into Southampton Buildings. Continue to Chancery Lane, where, on the corner on the right, are the London Silver Vaults. These are open to the public all day from Monday to Friday and also on Saturday mornings. Well below street level are corridors lined by shops with massive steel doors housing such vast displays of silverware that you could imagine yourself in an Aladdin's cave. As well as buying silverware you can also store your valuables here.

Down Chancery Lane to the left is the Public Record Office where important items of the state archives are kept, although many have now been removed to Kew. There is a small museum open Mondays–Fridays, 1–4. The glory of the collection is the Domesday Book, the first recorded item, in two vellum volumes, of market research in this country, ordered twenty years after his successful conquest, by William I, as a survey of all property in his domain. The popular name Domesday, which means Day of Judgement, arose because there was no right of appeal against the figures it recorded which we today would call rateable values. The museum also has cases filled with seals, and charters, and letters signed by kings, queens, generals, statesmen, writers. Most of them are legible.

On leaving the Public Record Office enter Lincoln's Inn (where, of course, you have absolutely no right of way) by a gatehouse further up the street.

Some explanation of the Inns of Court is necessary. Inn suggests hospitality or at the least accommodation: Court suggests law. In the Middle Ages when the practice of the law became separated from the clergy the inns evolved as colleges for intending lawyers, offices for those practising law and courtrooms in which the law was administered. Lincoln's Inn is the oldest of the Courts with records dating back to 1422. The other three are the Middle Temple (1501), the Inner Temple (1505) and Gray's Inn (1569).

The Inns no longer have Courts but they are still very much the training-grounds for those studying law and provide offices for those practising it. There are three tiers of membership: benchers, barristers and students. A student qualifies to become a barrister by passing the required examinations and by dining in the hall of the Inn a statutory number of times. He is then called to the Bar and may practise in the courts. The most eminent of barristers are made benchers of their Inn and on election they are required to contribute 'a substantial sum into the funds of the Inn as a fine on election' (a nice use of the word 'fine').

The requirement to dine in hall for would-be barristers is the surviving ritual for 'living in'. Historically the Inns provided all the necessities of life, rooms in which to live, a hall for dining, a chapel for worship, a library for study. All are extant and, in the case of Lincoln's Inn, the sixteenth-century old hall escaped the blitz as did the seventeenth-century chapel.

Attached to the Inns of Court were the Inns of Chancery of which Staple Inn (which we have just visited) was one. Historically they were Inns to which would-be barristers gravitated to train in the law before obtaining admission to an Inn of Court. Later they were bypassed by intending barristers and became the training-ground for solicitors. The latter formed themselves in the early nineteenth century into the Law Society and after this the Inns of Chancery declined in importance. Today both solicitors and barristers have their chambers in Lincoln's Inn, but people from other professions also work and live here.

Dickens worked in Lincoln's Inn, briefly, as a boy and it made a lasting impression. He formed an unfavourable opinion of the legal profession which he expressed throughout his writing life, but even his invective left the lawyers unmoved in their mighty power. Indeed, why should it not, since in so many cases it is lawyers inside parliament who make the laws. What is astonishing is that there should be so many amiable and likeable people working in this profession, and yet so many objectionable laws.

We leave for one last cultural experience in adjacent Lincoln's Inn Fields, on the north side of which is Sir John Soane's Museum. You never saw the like. Here in a long terrace of houses from various periods is the most eccentric collection in London. There is some hint of this if you study the exterior. Lying between two run-of-the-mill early nineteenth-century houses, ordinarily elegant after their own fashion — and what a fashion it was — is another, three bays wide. It has been rusticated at the ground floor, given a stony balcony with art-nouveau windows at the first and has stone figures, unprotected by balconies, about to step off the third. In this house architect Sir John Soane lived, cramming it with any and every item of treasure which took his fancy as he travelled the world, or which he could acquire through salerooms or private purchase. So in a typical Georgian-style terrace house he accumulated sufficient exhibits to satisfy the curator of a museum with thirty spacious galleries to fill. It is a fantastic collection of classical remains, heads, pediments, columns, sculptures, cornices, ceilings, fireplaces, urns, statues, friezes, furniture, jewellery. The basement has become a crypt littered with tombs, and every corridor and passage is packed with treasures. As you move between them holding your clothing firmly to you lest you crash some priceless object to the floor, you gasp in amazement at this wonderland of high-level junk. It is as though you have stumbled upon an antiques fair which closed down suddenly when a volcano erupted, and has been protected by lava for a century. Only a century, because I must not give the impression that the collection is confined to the classical world. There are paintings, books, furniture, decorations and so on from the Renaissance until about 1830. Soane built the houses on either side of his own, which is preserved as this remarkable museum, and not all of which has the ambience of a junk-shop. The dining-room is elegance itself with a table set for eight: how one would love to dine here.

There is no charge for admission: you must just sign the Visitors' Book. Then, when you have had your fill, return into Lincoln's Inn Fields, which is not a meadow but a typical London square with benches, tennis-courts and a tea-house.

Walk Two

Bank – Leadenhall Market – Lime Street –
The Tower of London – St Katharine's Dock – Monument –
London Bridge – Southwark Cathedral – Bankside –
Blackfriars – St Bride's – Temple – The Law Courts –
Lincoln's Inn Fields

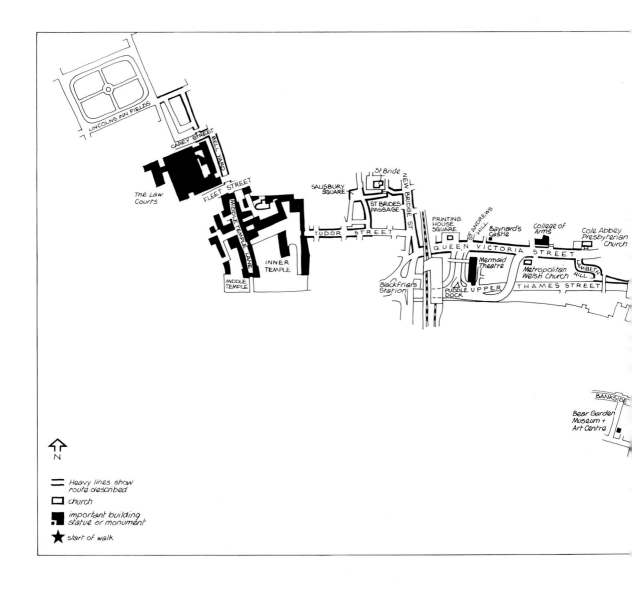

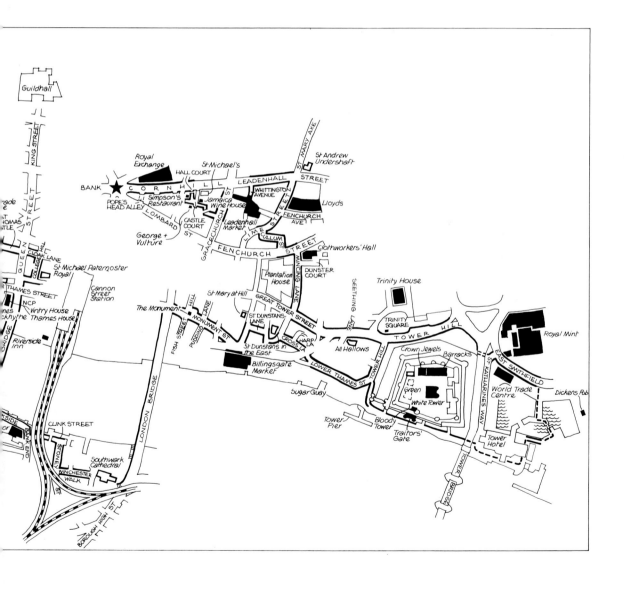

Leave Bank station by an exit for Cornhill – there are two. If you come up by the one on the left you will see, silhouetted against the light at the top of the steps, a handsome clock protruding from the side of the Royal Exchange. Cross Cornhill, and you will scarcely be aware that it is a hill, but it was to the Romans, the surface of whose city lies well below your feet. You will pass Pope's Head Alley and other narrow lanes running through to Lombard Street. The man who knows his City treats these as shortcuts and moves swiftly along them. Everyone in the City is in a hurry. Time is money, and money counts. The visitor will probably get lost without a large-scale map. You may wish to go through to Lombard Street, just to say you have seen the centre of banking, a slightly winding dingy street where the Lombards, from Italy, put up their trading signs after the expulsion of the Jews. Modern versions of some of the signs may still be seen and they are about the only items of interest, although there is the church of St Edmund the King, unremarkable by City standards but unlucky in having suffered not only from 1666 and 1940 but also from First World War bombs.

Return to Cornhill and observe the wrought-iron doorway on the side of the Royal Exchange, the decoration above and beside it, and the surrounding windows. Stone fruits and flowers riot: grapes and passion flowers are in particular abundance. In these stark architectural times one grasps gratefully at anything which breaks the monotony. Turn right into Ball Court where you will find Simpson's Restaurant (Tavern) tucked into a corner. Walk on to Castle Court, facing the back of the George and Vulture, which brings us again to Dickensland. The George and Vulture is partly eighteenth-century and there are a few other buildings hereabouts which also survive from that time. Mr Pickwick tippled at the George & V., and the City Pickwick Club still holds meetings there. I once attended a subscription lunch in the top-floor dining-room where we had roast beef of old England washed down with the claret of old Bordeaux. Cedric Dickens, great-grandson of the writer, rallied the assembled booksellers to declare how many copies they would buy of an edition of *A Christmas Carol* which he was publishing in aid of the house in Doughty Street (see Walk Six). Until the late nineteenth century books were often sold in this way. I am glad the custom has died out. One's judgement is not at its best when hospitality is as lavish as it was that day at the George and Vulture.

In St Michael's Alley, off Castle Court, there is the Jamaica Wine House on the site of the Pasqua Rossee's Head which, in 1652, was London's first coffee house. The severe partitioned interior is not, to me, attractive, nor was the small glass of lukewarm white wine I

Mr Pickwick's pub
The George & Vulture
Castle Court

bought there for 77p, but some serious drinkers rate it highly. St Michael's refers to the church on Cornhill which is on a very ancient site where a Saxon church once stood. The present building is mainly Victorian and little of the work of Wren and Hawksmoor is to be seen thanks to the improvements imposed upon it by Sir George Gilbert Scott. It is not easy to see it anyway because the building density here is intense. Ironically, it came through the blitz unscathed.

Make your way through to Gracechurch Street – and you will probably have to flag down a passing businessman to ask the way – and turn left, before crossing it to go into Leadenhall Market where the Roman basilica, the centre of commercial life, once stood. It is a cavernous Victorian structure laid out crosswise with shops, stalls, pubs and cafés lining the two streets. It started as a poultry market but now you can buy almost anything there. It makes a welcome contrast from what we have seen, and from what is to come, and once again the route is difficult to describe. If you get lost ask to be directed to the Tower and skip the next few paragraphs. Around Leadenhall Street, which is reached from Whittington Street, enormous developments are under way and even what is or is not a street is in doubt. In Leadenhall itself massive transformations have already occurred. One mostly glass tower is the P&O building (shipping is this street's theme) and standing beside it is an even more monstrous erection. CU, it proclaims itself, which means Commercial Union Assurance. At its lowest visible point, sprouting from the pavement, as though announcing a submerged loo, is something called The Underwriter. Actually it is a pub.

A rare survivor from the distant past, across St Mary Axe, is the church of St Andrew Undershaft. And a survivor it is because it escaped almost entirely the ravages of both 1666 and 1940. John Stow, London's first historian, worshipped here, and there is a monument to him within. He died in 1605. On the anniversary of his death in April each year the quill pen on his statue is renewed and the Lord Mayor presents a copy of his history to the writer of the best essay on London submitted during the previous twelve months. An undershaft was a maypole which used to be erected in front of the south door on the appropriate day. In 1517, as Stow relates, this led to a riot against foreign apprentices, who, it was thought, were depriving the natives of work. As a result use of the undershaft was forbidden but, according to Stow, it became an 'idol'. In 1549 it was the subject of a passionate sermon delivered at 'Paules cross', the aftermath of which was that the citizens 'sawed it in pieces' and then burned them.

Cross Leadenhall Street again into Lime Street. On the corner of Fenchurch Avenue, as anonymous as any Pall Mall club, is Lloyd's, the premier centre of insurance which began in Edward Lloyd's coffee house in Great Tower Street in the 1680s. Lloyd gathered news from his mercantile customers and when he moved to Lombard Street, in 1691, his premises became the unofficial home of marine insurance. Today Lloyd's is a society of members who use their own money to underwrite whatever seems to them a good risk, but they no longer confine themselves to shipping. Before becoming a member an aspiring underwriter must give proof of very substantial liquid assets. He then becomes part of a syndicate which must pay up when an aircraft costing millions crashes into a hillside or when a ship goes down. In the underwriting room is the Lutine Bell which is rung once when a ship is lost, and twice if it was in danger but has come through it.

Continue along Lime Street until you reach Cullum Street where you see a good example of how an old City alley has been all but destroyed, not by war but by development. A quarter of a century ago it was still a slip-through with right-angled entries from Fenchurch and Lime Streets, and was lined with little shops. Now one side has been replaced by a high-rise block, the right angle into Fenchurch Street has been widened and another block set back from it. Cullum Street still had some air of romance about it when I worked near by in 1956. Now it has none.

Cross Fenchurch Street at Plantation House, a neo-classical edifice spreading far into Mincing Lane, into which you turn right. Mincing, according to Stow, means 'the lane of the nuns', but what those ladies were doing here has never been satisfactorily explained and there is no sign of them today. Nor is there any building earlier than 1900. In Dunster Court, reached through a wrought-iron gate with gold leaf upon it, is Clothworkers' Hall. At the end of the Lane turn left into Great Tower Street for a first view of the Tower of London which can be seen beyond the church of All Hallows. We cross to the latter by a subway near Seething Lane where Samuel Pepys worked in the Navy Office, and also lived. It was here that he first observed the great fire. All Hallows was saved because houses standing close to it were destroyed to prevent the flames spreading. In 1940, however, it was almost totally ruined. The bombs disclosed the arch of a Saxon church which has been dated to AD 675 when the abbey of Barking, a few miles down river on the Essex bank, and founded by Erkenwald, Bishop of London, held land here. This is why the church is referred to as All Hallows, Barking-by-the-Tower. It has been expertly restored with a wide, light interior and clear east windows above the altar. It is a church with a maritime theme, the south chapel being known as the Mariners'. There are votive model ships and the baptistery was the gift of a naval officer: its font is of Gibraltar limestone carved by a Sicilian prisoner of war. Its cover is a restored piece by Grinling Gibbons.

All Hallows is also the church of Toc H, a movement started by Tubby Clayton (vicar from 1922 to 1963) when he was an army chaplain in the First World War. It began as a fellowship of men and women in an attic chapel at Talbot House in Poperinghe, near Ypres. The initials of Talbot House in signallers' language are Toc H, to learn which detracts from the mystery of the name.

You should certainly visit the crypt of All Hallows and you may be fortunate in being conducted through it by a man named Frank who has an immense and deep love of London and its history, and especially of this church. He will show you, with something of a proprietorial air, the Roman mosaic excavated in 1928 and thought to be the floor of a late second-century house. He will discourse knowledgeably and amiably about a model of Roman London of AD 400, a Saxon cross, the oratory of St Clare, a seventeenth-century burial vault, and the church registers detailing, in legible handwriting, the frequent burial services during times of plague. He will also ask you questions and prise answers out of you with the skill of a born teacher. There is much else of interest in the church including a brass-rubbing centre, examples of wrought-iron sword rests and windows of partially stained glass dedicated to the Port of London Authority and the Tower of London.

The Port of London Authority building, 'a lasting monument to Edwardian optimism' (Pevsner), is off Trinity Square, but it is now the offices of an insurance company. London still has docks but as a port is much diminished because a lot of what was unloaded by the Thames now reaches the country in container trucks. What still comes in ships needs deeper water and is catered for at Tilbury Docks, about 24 miles east of Tower Bridge. The PLA still controls the river but its task is different from when Sir Edwin Cooper designed a classical palace for its headquarters.

Next to it is a restored late-eighteenth-century house which David Piper describes as being as 'austere and controlled as a cool rose-bud' beside a 'monstrous wedding-cake'. Trinity House is the headquarters of the Brethren of the Trinity who control lightships, buoys, lighthouses and pilots, and work in close cooperation with the Royal Navy.

From All Hallows we move on to Tower Hill, a pitch for outdoor orators who attract lunchtime crowds on fine days. It leads down to the entrance to the Tower which is, of course, a 'must'. Try to dissociate it from the dreadful crimes committed within its walls if you can, and assess it as a building. As such it was nothing if not

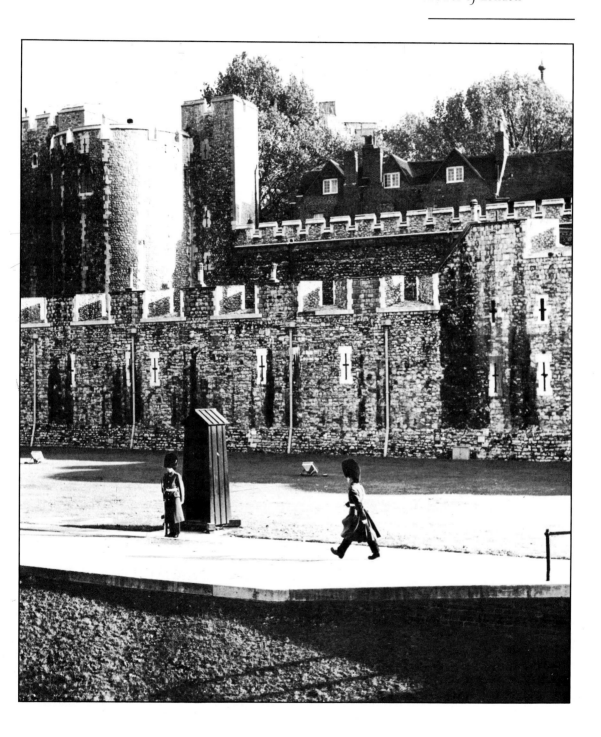

practical so it has to be accepted as a prison and a fortress. As a home, according to one of those quaintly dressed Beefeaters who lives there with his family, it can be depressing.

William the Conqueror built the White Tower just within the Roman city. Its walls, of Caen stone, are between 15 and 11 feet thick, and in the thirteenth century it was whitewashed. It has a banqueting hall, a council chamber, a chapel, sword room and vaults. Until the coming of high explosives it was truly impregnable. It speaks of tremendous strength of purpose, and is not for the timid or the weak. The chapel of St John, on the second floor, is severe, even primitive – a place in which brave knights can pray for victory to a God who must surely be on their side. It is an awesome chamber emphasizing the austerity of the entire keep around which battles have never actually raged. Over the centuries other towers have been added and there is now a complex of buildings within the moat. This was drained in 1843. Some of it is grassed and is used as playing-fields by the garrison. Henry III, Richard I and Edward I all enlarged the fortress, building more walls and towers (there are eighteen in all), amongst them the one named Bloody, where Sir Walter Raleigh spent thirteen years of imprisonment, where Cranmer and Archbishop Laud were confined and where the little princes are supposed to have been murdered. All the towers have had distinguished residents. Some, such as Queen Elizabeth I, were freed. She, in due course, incarcerated others here. A famous legend surrounds the Bowyer Tower where Prince Clarence was said to have drowned in a barrel of malmsey, a story which appeals to many Englishmen because it has 'oh, what a lovely death' undertones. Anne Boleyn, Guy Fawkes and countless others were brought here through Traitors' Gate, up the steps from the river, to await their summons to the executioner's axe. One of the last (although not by that entrance) was the fleeing Nazi, Rudolf Hess, who was spared to endure a lifetime of imprisonment elsewhere.

Although there are dwellings and offices within the walls the Tower is in no way domesticated. It is haunted by its frightful history, and the ravens are to me symbols of the savagery which pervades the place. These fine birds with their rich glossy black feathers have their wings clipped so that they cannot fly away, because legend has it that the Tower will not survive if it loses them. I find this mutilation obscene even though it is said that only birds already sick or injured are subjected to it.

The Crown Jewels are here and there is usually a long queue of people waiting to see them in the upper and lower chambers of Waterloo Barracks. To the east of Wakefield Tower there is a history gallery with models of the whole complex in 1547 and 1866. In the White Tower there are displays of armour including that worn by Henry VIII on ceremonial occasions, perhaps on the Field of the Cloth of Gold. There are many galleries within the White Tower devoted to different aspects of war and armour, sport and tournaments. In the Bowyer, lest you have not had enough of man's brutality to man, there is a collection of instruments of torture and punishment, including a block and axe.

At the chapel of St Peter-ad-Vincula to the north-west of the White Tower, beheaded queens and dukes lie buried, along with poor Lady Jane Grey who was queen for only a few days. Below it, on Tower Green, she was executed. So were Anne Boleyn and Catherine Howard. St Peter is flanked by the Queen's House from which Lord Nithsdale, condemned to the block, escaped dressed as a woman in 1716. He was part of a Stuart rebellion which came to nought. Had it succeeded would he have sent others to die here? I don't like the Tower. It is an evil place provoking gloomy thoughts. I hate what it stands for but admire it as a building, the White Tower especially. Is it so arresting because the builders believed in what they were doing as they moved the blocks of Caen stone into position, whereas the operators of cranes above modern building sites do not as they manoeuvre their girders?

No such thoughts are sparked off by the sight of Tower Bridge, an ingenious example of Victorian engineering which enables ships to pass through without much interruption to the traffic flow across the Thames. It is loved by David Piper who calls it 'a rather warming impression of London's pride' and 'the city's trademark'. Pevsner disapproves: 'The massive structure does much damage to the skyline of the City, and the apparent scale of the Tower.' V. S. Pritchett, in *London Perceived*, fantasizes about it and wavers between the two: 'it became ... the symbol of the city', or 'in some moods one feels the whole thing is some owlish and baronial fake from a German baronry', yet 'seen in the kindness of fog or mist (it) has the beauty of a heavy web hung from the sky'.

Once, in the 1960s, there was drama when the bridge's movable inner section began to rise with a bus already on it. The driver was praised for his quick decision in accelerating and making it over the gap. If he had reversed it is likely that his passengers would have been injured or killed. (But why wasn't the operator looking?)

Tower Bridge is the last down-river on the Thames. I prefer the simplicity of Waterloo but that is a road bridge under which only low craft can pass. It was necessary to make Tower Bridge openable for the convenience of bigger ships which until the 1950s still docked at

Tower Bridge

wharfs in the Pool of London (between London and Tower Bridges). Like it or no it is a most efficient piece of workmanship and it is said that it has never failed to open. The pedestrian way over the top had to be closed, however, when it became popular for attempted suicide. It can now be walked again on payment of a fee which entitles you also to view a machine room and two exhibitions. But, no leaping.

We go under a section of Tower Bridge which is on land, past a man roasting chestnuts, to St Katharine's Way which leads to the Tower Hotel. The brown biscuit-coloured glass and concrete frontage faces the Thames across an embankment which has the delightful sculpture by David Wynne, *Girl with a Dolphin*. (His *Boy with a Dolphin* is in Cheyne Walk, Chelsea.) Opposite, the frontage of the south bank is unkempt with old warehouses, many of them derelict, as were the ones this side until a few years ago. The dock had fallen into disuse and the once functional buildings which served it were crumbling. Then the World Trade Centre was built with a hotel to accommodate those using it. The dock itself became a mooring-place for private yachts and a site for the Historic Ships Museum. One warehouse became a pub, the Dickens Inn, others were turned into shops and restaurants. There is also the London Seamanship School. It is an area which has been most successfully resurrected and the star attraction, for me and many others, is the Museum in which Scott's *Discovery* is the principal exhibit. It was moved here from the Victoria Embankment but may not remain for long. When I board it I get a feeling of horror at what it must have been like to be marooned on this vessel in the Antarctic ice for two years as Scott and his colleagues were. The museum is run by the Maritime Trust which is dedicated to rescuing and restoring vessels of historical interest, so here are light ships and tugs and dirty British coasters, and a turn-of-the-century Thames barge, most of which you are permitted to visit. There is a charge for admission.

Leave the dock, which was designed by Telford, by the exit in East Smithfield and turn left past the World Trade Centre, whose negative exterior is brightened by the fluttering flags of many nations. Opposite is the Royal Mint, heavily protected behind walls and railings. Until 1809 the Mint was inside the Tower walls; now it lies in the Greater London Borough of Tower Hamlets, formerly Stepney, but minting goes on elsewhere.

Cross St Katharine's Way and walk on the pavement above the Tower, or descend into its outer gardens, from which there is an underpass. This leads to another piece of Roman wall (one bit is very much like another) and to Trinity Gardens where there is a monument to the merchant seamen and fishermen lost at sea in World War Two. Return to Tower Hill and walk down it for the second time to Lower Thames Street where there is a pier from which you can take excursion boats down to Greenwich or up river, changing at Westminster, to Hampton Court. (There are royal palaces at both places but they do not come within the scope of these walks.) There is little else of interest in this street apart from the name Sugar

Quay, the home of Tate and Lyle, so hurry on into Cross Lane, through Harp Lane, from which you approach the ruined church of St Dunstan-in-the-East. The tower stands and is now a private chapel for the Vicar of All Hallows, but what remains of the nave is a shell of walls covered with trailing plants. It has been converted into an award-winning garden where City workers may relax at lunchtime, but it is also intended to be a lasting reminder of what happened in the blitz. At the end of St Dunstan's Lane you see another church, St Mary-at-Hill, which has seventy-two intact box pews, a pulpit with an elaborate wooden staircase and an attractive projecting clock on its outside. Turn back to Lower Thames Street where Billingsgate fish market stood for centuries and then bear right into Monument Street, past a pub called the Walrus and the Carpenter. The Monument is Wren's work and commemorates the Great Fire which started, as every schoolchild knows, at a house in nearby Pudding Lane. It is a Doric column 202 feet high and you may climb its 311 steps up a spiral staircase to reach a railinged balcony from which there is said to be a super view. I confess I have never enjoyed it, even as a boy, and don't ever expect to. Wren wanted a less solemn memorial with flickering flames in brass creeping up the sides but perhaps it is as well that this was overruled. There is a sculpture on the base, however, by Cibber, showing the fire still burning while rebuilding has already started, and the King, dressed as a Roman of course, observing it.

Cross Fish Street Hill to turn left on to London Bridge which for centuries was the only one across the river. It was replaced many times. The most famous one, again as all schoolkids know, had houses and shops and a chapel on it and was as picturesque as the Ponte Vecchio. Its nineteen narrow arches made it tricky for navigators when there was a strong current and also contributed to a phenomenon which has not occurred since 1814 – the freezing over of the Thames. On one occasion when this happened a famous frost fair was held and an ox roasted on the ice. That was in 1683/4; there is a memorable description of the river under these conditions in Virginia Woolf's *Orlando*. The houses on the bridge were taken down in the eighteenth century, the bridge itself in 1832. Its successor lasted until 1971 when it was replaced by the present bridge, with wider pavements to take the crowds which pour across it on working mornings and back on working evenings. (The old bridge was bought by some Americans.) Cross by the west side because it is difficult to do so at the other end and we are going over to visit Southwark Cathedral and Bankside where Shakespeare's Globe and other Elizabethan theatres stood.

*202 ft from Pudding Lane
The base of Wren's
Monument*

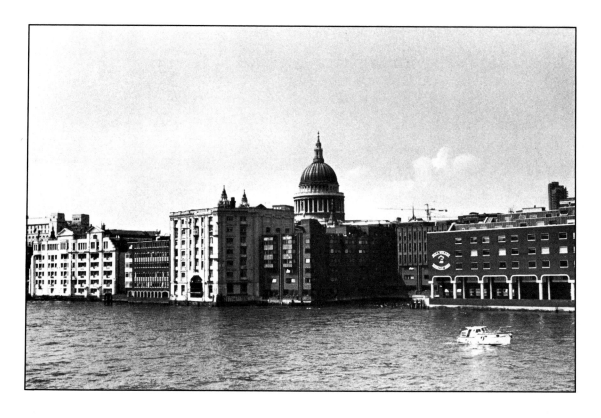

Thames wharfs
from London Bridge

No other cathedral I can think of is quite so shamefully positioned as Southwark, which looks as though it was jettisoned into an odd space which happened not to be needed for roads and railway tracks. Of course, the cathedral was there first, although it wasn't classified as such until 1905. A priory was on the site in the twelfth century but it was burned down in the thirteenth. A church took its place and was in a ruinous condition for most of the next five hundred years or so, until its restoration in 1822. It is a great mixture of styles but the experts say its design is basically thirteenth-century. There is a splendid stone screen behind the altar and an air of wellbeing pervades the nave as though the present custodians are making up for the neglect of centuries. The outside is grubby but what else can be expected with trains trundling above it on viaducts and the traffic grinding past? The particular attraction for me, and I do not find it at all a moving building as I do the great Gothic cathedrals, is the Shakespeare Memorial Window. There are three arched panels of stained glass depicting characters from the plays, the Seven Ages of Man and a centrepiece of Prospero, with Caliban grovelling beneath him, freeing Ariel. Underneath it is an effigy of Shakespeare recumbent, head resting on hand and elbow, in front of a frieze of

Stoney Street
Southwark (opposite)

Bankside. There is also a tomb to John Trehearne, Gentleman Porter to King James I. Road and railway builders have permitted the retention of a small garden.

You should be able to leave by Cathedral Street but it is blocked because of rebuilding. Minerva House looks interesting, with alternating thin strips of glass and yellow ochre brick at varying heights. It gives one hope that we may have come through the worst that contemporary architects can do. So you leave by Winchester Walk, but before going, a word or two about Southwark which is as old as London itself. There were Romans here at the southern end of their bridge, and there are associations with Geoffrey Chaucer whose Canterbury pilgrims set forth on their momentous journey after assembling at the Tabard Inn. It is no longer there but part of the George, a late-seventeenth-century hostelry with a galleried court-yard, is in the Borough High Street. Despite the depredations of railway companies, who are responsible for claiming its northern side, it is still maintained by the National Trust as a working inn. But we go into a seedy area of warehouses and building sites, right into Stoney Street, left into Clink Street and under the railway bridge which takes trains into and out of Cannon Street station. There is a plaque telling about the Clink Prison which stood hereabouts and contributed a word to the language. Religious martyrs, some precursors of the Pilgrim Fathers, were incarcerated here and many were later hanged and mutilated elsewhere.

Then you face Bank End where there is a pretty pub, the Anchor, with an outdoors extension overlooking the Thames. It is really all there is here at the moment and, as pubs do, it will no doubt survive to be surrounded by high office blocks. There is a way through to Southwark Bridge, and a sign to the Bear Gardens Museum and Arts Centre, which has a full-size working model of the Cockpit Theatre (1616). Also, according to the Blue Guide to *Museums and Galleries of London*, models of the Globe and the Swan and much else of interest to students of the Elizabethan theatre, but I have been unable to find it open. I hope it will regain its place in the community as the area is developed.

Back then to the north bank across Southwark Bridge ignoring, so far as one can, the frightful rail bridge to Cannon Street and the station itself with its two dirty towers and unroofed platforms. At the end of Southwark which, like Tower Bridge, is painted blue, is the Riverside Inn on the right and a pleasant line of low building above the mudflats. On the left are Vintry House and Thames House, both ponderously neo-classical and facing a National Car Park in twentieth-century Corrugated.

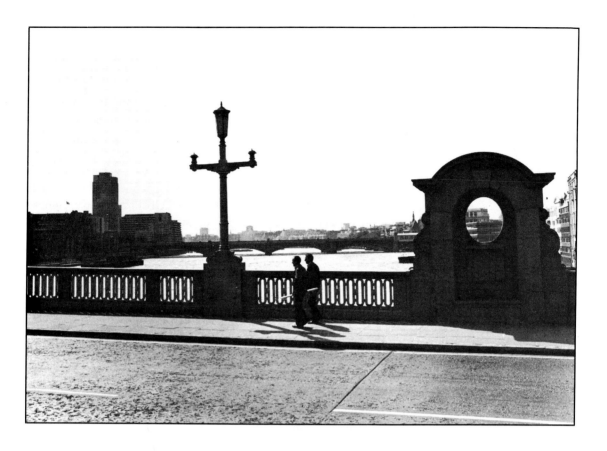

At Upper Thames Street note the view of the Guildhall seen at the end of King Street, but bear right for a few steps before crossing to St Michael, Paternoster Royal, which is the church of Sir Richard Whittington. Somewhere beside or beneath it is his tomb but it has been lost in the various devastations suffered over the centuries since his death in 1423. St Michael's now houses the Mission to Seamen. On leaving turn right up College Hill where Whittington is remembered on a plaque stating that he founded the church, and also in a wine bar at No. 21. Then go left into Cloak Lane opposite (in Queen Street) the splendid pair of eighteenth-century houses now both numbered 28. They are two of the very few remaining in the City and are used as offices for a partnership of chartered surveyors. There is a small neatly kept garden in front of them. Beside them is Great St Thomas Apostle, a street, not a deified priest, which leads into the heart of the fur trade with nameplates such as David Nagioff, Highcraft Trading Company, Afghan Embroidered Sheepskins. The City may veer towards a lack of variety architecturally but its detail is endlessly fascinating.

Southwark Bridge and River Thames to the west

Turn left into Garlick Hill towards St James Garlickhythe. The church has a typically light Wren interior with one unfussy chandelier hanging from a ceiling in gold and white. On a pillar is stated: 'Sir Christopher Wren He Builded This Church Ob.1727'. It has one of the great man's most joyful towers with pillars, pinnacles, lantern, weathervane and cross mounting triumphantly above each other. The Music for the Royal Fireworks should always be playing when you look at it.

A ramp leads down to Upper Thames Street with Fur Trade House on the right. This is an especially beastly part of London, so I shall urge you on quickly. Where there is an isolated church tower without a church (as occurs not infrequently) turn right up Lambeth Hill into Queen Victoria Street opposite Cole Abbey Presbyterian Church (formerly St Nicholas Cole) which looks like a city hall with steeple attached. This is because Wren was ever anxious to bring light into his churches and happy to settle for a simple oblong with large clear windows.

Queen Victoria Street, for the pedestrian, is little improvement on Upper Thames but there are steps here and there leading to St Paul's to distract you from the traffic, and also the College of Arms, a seventeenth-century house in a courtyard. Here Garter King at Arms presides over matters heraldic and genealogical, so if you are worried about aspects of your ancestry you should attend here and let gentlemen with exotic names like Rouge Croix and Rouge Dragon solve your problems. For a fee, they are qualified to do so. On the opposite side is what is now the Metropolitan Welsh Church but was St Benet, Paul's Wharf, which is evidence of Wren's versatility and foresight. How could he have known that this brick hall, surely a model for so much nineteenth-century industrial architecture of the pumping station variety, would be a perfect home for Welsh Episcopalianism? The tower with a small dome and lantern, only very slightly facetious, stands at one corner, the Norman windows have little decorative squiggles above them like eyebrows, the brickwork at the corners of the tower and nave are picked out in liquorice allsort pattern. Within, services, look you, are conducted in the Welsh language.

Near the western end of Upper Thames Street there is the Continental Bank House where once stood Blackfriars Hall, and later Printing House Square. The Hall was where Henry VIII pleaded with a Papal Court to be allowed to divorce Anne Boleyn. *The Times* newspaper occupied Printing House Square until it moved, a few years ago, to Gray's Inn Road. Blackfriars as a name derives, obviously, from a monastery. Now it is a district not at all well

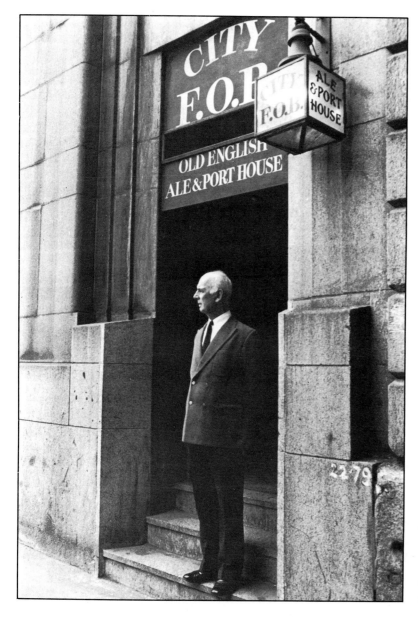

Ale and Port Bar
Queen Victoria Street

defined and has a station which used to be more romantic when it had on its stone fascia the names of far-away destinations such as St Petersburg. (They are now preserved inside.) Nor is the Mermaid Theatre so attractively situated as it was when Bernard Miles gave the city its only playhouse in the 1950s. Puddle Dock, which is still its address, has been sacrificed to the new road system but a theatre is still there although difficult to locate. Almost opposite, on the corner

of St Andrew's Hill, is a pub called Baynard's Castle. This commemorates the site, near by, of a long since demolished Norman fortress. Under its remains there have been many archaeological finds. It will be difficult to concentrate on such matters as you cross New Bridge Street where and when you can to the comparative calm of St Bride's Passage leading to the church of the same name, more popularly known as the wedding-cake church. If there is one spire in London more delightful than all others it is this one. The only question arising is, which came first, the spire or the wedding-cake? Happily, Wren's frivolity survived the blitz when the church itself was burned out. It has been rebuilt with the usual care and there is a crypt as interesting as All Hallows'. In it can be seen fragments of Roman and medieval wall and a museum recording one thousand years of history because St Bride's, formerly St Bridget's, is one of the oldest London churches. It has long associations with the written and printed word. Caxton's successor and pupil, Wynkyn de Worde, who moved his master's press from Westminster to Fleet Street, is buried here. It is surrounded by newspaper offices and one press baron's son, Sir Max Aitken, paid for the restoration of the crypt in memory of his father, Lord Beaverbrook. It is perhaps also appropriate that it should be known as the journalists' church because the Irish St Bridget, after whom it was first named, is alleged to have been capable of making well water change into beer. Now there's a foine Christian deed to warm the cockles of a reporter's heart.

From religion and literature, if the latter is a proper word to use in Fleet Street, to religion and the law. From St Bride's go through Salisbury Square, one of London's smallest, down into Tudor Street and along to the Temple. Not Temple *of* anything, but another of the Inns of Court, or rather two of them because there is an Inner and a Middle Temple (but no Outer). There is also a church because the name derives from the Knights Templar, a crusading order who fought constantly against Islam and built round Norman churches. Eventually they lost favour with popes and kings and their temple here was taken over by lawyers after the order was suppressed at the start of the fourteenth century. So here it is now the largest of the Inns, with many courts, gardens, walks and halls, a library, a treasury and cloisters. As with Lincoln's and Gray's Inn there is a calm within the Temple, but although it is part of the City it is also separate from it. It is subject to the laws of Britain, it could even be said that it makes them, but it is also a law unto itself. It is both private and public property. No one will stop you from entering or leaving, if you behave decently, but you have absolutely no right to be here, unless you are a member of Inner or Middle Temple or dwell here. It is very English

The Black Friar of Blackfriars (opposite)

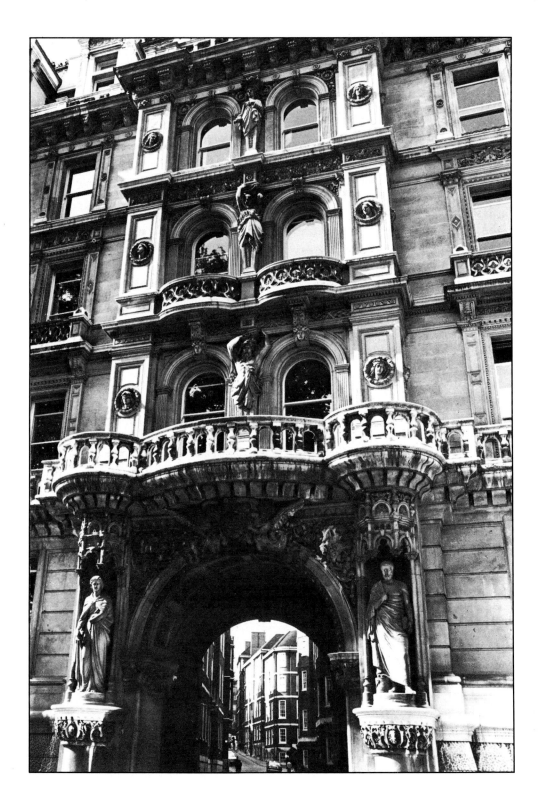

and typical of the law. Wander about it, enjoy the atmosphere and when you have had enough, and are beginning to feel the mould growing on the insides of your shoes, come out into busy Fleet Street by Middle Temple Lane, browse in my friend Lou Simmond's bookshop, or climb up to Prince Henry's Room which is next door on the first floor of an early seventeenth-century house that has been well preserved in its timbering and ceiling. It is not known to have any actual connection with the son of James I apart from having his initials carved on the ceiling. It is open on weekday afternoons.

Here you are at the western edge of the City where Temple Bar once stood as a gateway. It is now on an estate in Hertfordshire but there is a move to return it, although not to this actual site where it would certainly impede traffic flow. Here, also, are the Law Courts, heavily Gothic in character and representing to me, in their intricate design, both inside and out, the almost incomprehensible nature of the law. My instincts in this respect are entirely Dickensian. At some time in our lives most of us have had to attend at the Law Courts, where only civil cases are heard. It has happened to me only once and I was not convinced that the proceedings resulted in justice being done. (I was neither plaintiff nor defendant, only witness.)

In search of a green place in which to end the walk we must go again into Lincoln's Inn Fields. We go by Bell Yard, Carey Street (a name indelibly connected with bankruptcy) and under an arch to the Inn itself where we savour that ambience of peace in which lawyers like to envelop themselves. The Fields, as we already know, are a planned square. It is one of London's many lungs and in it, whilst we are enjoying welcome cups of tea, we may reflect that we are out of the City and in that other London which we shall meet on our walks from Trafalgar Square.

Middle Temple Lane
(opposite)

Walk Three

Trafalgar Square – The Mall – Buckingham Palace –
The Queen's Gallery – Eaton Square – Belgrave Square –
Sloane Square – Knightsbridge – The V&A –
Exhibition Road – The Albert Hall –
Kensington Palace and Gardens

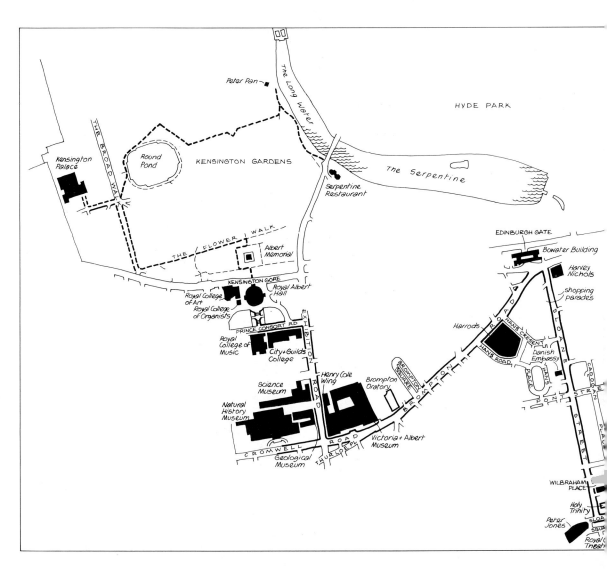

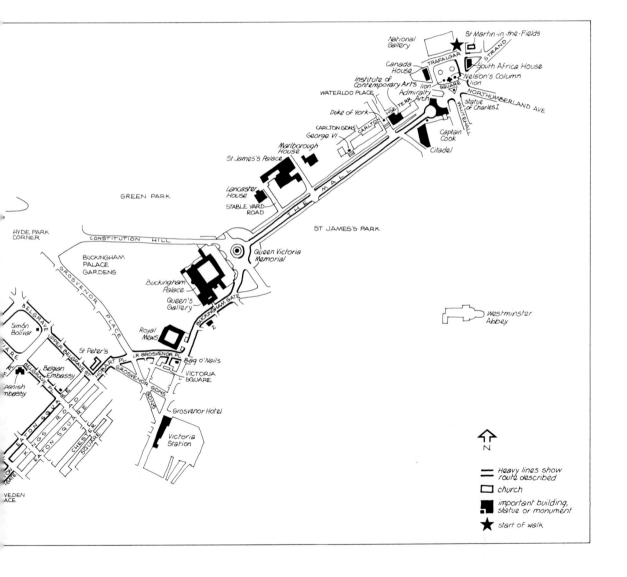

St Martin-in-the-Fields
National Gallery
STRAND
Canada House
South Africa House
Institute of Contemporary Arts
Nelson's Column
lion
Waterloo Place
Admiralty Arch
lion
NORTHUMBERLAND AVE
TRAFALGAR SQUARE
Duke of York
statue of Charles I
CARLTON GDNS
George VI
WHITEHALL
Captain Cook
Marlborough House
St James's Palace
Citadel
Lancaster House
STABLE YARD ROAD
GREEN PARK
THE MALL
ST JAMES'S PARK
HYDE PARK CORNER
CONSTITUTION HILL
Queen Victoria Memorial
BUCKINGHAM PALACE GARDENS
GROSVENOR PLACE
Buckingham Palace
BELGRAVE
Simón Bolívar
Buckingham Palace
Queen's Gallery
BUCKINGHAM GATE
Westminster Abbey
St Peter's
Royal Mews
LR GROSVENOR PL.
Bag o'Nails
Belgian Embassy
Spanish Embassy
VICTORIA SQUARE
GROSVENOR GDNS
Grosvenor Hotel
VEDEN ACE
Victoria Station

N

— Heavy lines show route described
☐ church
■ important building, statue or monument
★ start of walk

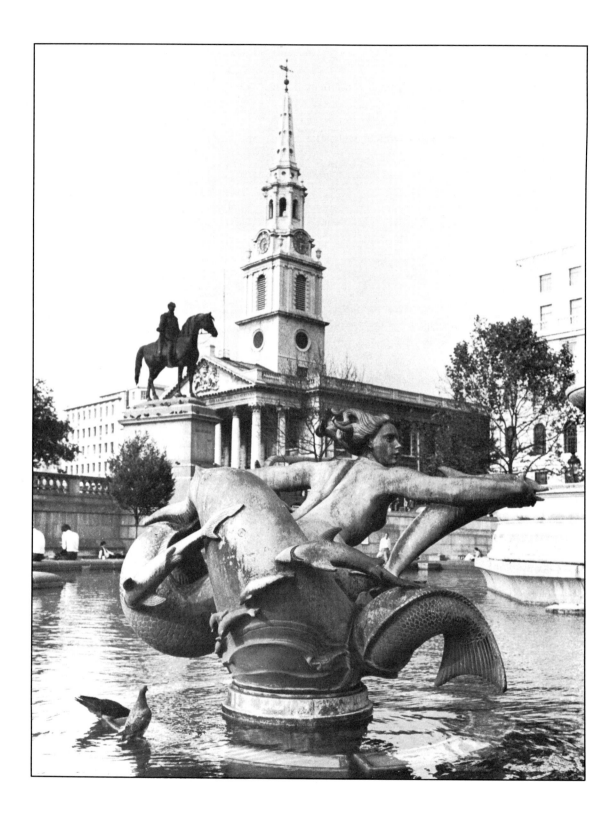

The first two walks start at Bank, the undoubted centre of the City; the other six begin in Trafalgar Square which is certainly not the centre of Westminster or of London. Parliament Square could claim to be that, although I have never heard it so described. In popular lore Piccadilly Circus is probably favourite but Trafalgar Square is 'my' centre for a series of walks which will take us to St James's, Kensington, Mayfair, the South Bank, Bloomsbury, Hyde Park, and Regent's Park.

Trafalgar, London's best-known square, was laid out in the 1820s. As a design it compares unfavourably with what most other European capitals can offer. There is little attempt at uniformity and on its south side it is frayed at the edges.

William Wilkins's neo-classical National Gallery on the north side should, but doesn't, dominate the square; what does take the eye from many directions is James Gibbs's church of St Martin-in-the-Fields with its temple frontage and Wren-style steeple soaring into the sky. This building, which isn't actually on it, alone gives the square distinction. Certainly the lifeless piles of Canada House and South Africa House, to west and east, do not, nor does shabby old Grand Buildings on the corner of Northumberland Avenue, though it is possible to perceive signs of life going on within it. (I have never seen anyone go in or out of the other two; probably they are inhabited only by security guards watching for movements beneath the dustsheets.)

What ought to dominate is Nelson's Column. This is what the square is supposed to be about and inasmuch as you are always aware of it looming above, it does, but you cannot actually look at it without permanently cricking your neck. And the only way of inspecting Nelson, 170 feet overhead, is with fieldglasses or by helicopter.

It would have needed the combined ruthlessness of a Napoleon and a Haussmann to make Trafalgar Square what it should have become, an inspired meeting of Whitehall, the Mall and the Strand, offering superb vistas of Westminster Abbey and Buckingham Palace. In fact John Nash's plans to honour the victor of Trafalgar included connecting roads to Regent Street and the British Museum but Parliament, at first enthusiastic for a new national memorial to our maritime greatness, grew parsimonious. So the square evolved in a piecemeal way and Nash had been dead for several years before Charles Barry levelled the slope to take the column. Nash did live to see the National Gallery (for which his designs were rejected) started upon but died in 1835 before its completion. Other buildings on the boundaries of the square, which was formerly occupied with the Royal Mews and mean dwelling houses, came later. All that remains

St Martin's and a Mermaid Trafalgar Square (opposite)

now from before the nineteenth century, apart from St Martin's, is the equestrian statue of Charles I facing towards the scene of his execution. It was hidden during the Civil War and placed there by Charles II who removed an Eleanor Cross to make way for it. (Eleanor, the Spanish-born Queen of Edward I, died of a fever near Nottingham. Her embalmed corpse was conveyed in solemn procession from Lincoln to Westminster. The sorrowing King had crosses erected at each stopping-place, the last of which was Charing at the top of Whitehall.)

So much for history. Probably most people would agree with the words of the popular ditty about a down-and-out who sleeps in Trafalgar Square and sings:

> I owns it's a trifle draughty,
> But I looks at it this way, yer see,
> If it's good ·enough for Nelson,
> Then it's quite good enough for me.

Londoners accept it for what it is, for the part it plays in their life. For many it is associated with revelry on New Year's Eve when (until 1983), in the shadow of the giant Christmas tree sent each year from Norway, foolhardy merrymakers leapt into the icy waters of the ponds below the fountains. For others it means Landseer's noble stone lions guarding the column, or, quite simply, popcorn for feeding the pigeons. For yet more it is demonstration territory, a prime site for expressions of dissent. From here the early Aldermaston marches against the use of nuclear weapons commenced. Here, traditionally, on Sunday afternoons politicians, usually in Opposition, climb on to the windswept plinth to inveigh against racism, war, factory farming, totalitarianism, religious and political persecution and the government of the day. The demonstrations used to be comparatively well behaved although cordons of police were usually in reserve to hold back the crowd if it showed signs of getting out of hand. On one occasion when arrests had already been made I heard a bobby, who was being moved to and fro in a human chain of policemen, as the crowd eddied this way and that, politely informing a young woman that the friend about whom she was inquiring was probably detained at Duncannon Street Police Station. Nowadays, there is more likelihood of violence.

On weekdays and most of Sundays the square presents a less frenzied scene. There is a lack of greenery but people find it pleasant to sit beside the water or on the steps, and to saunter past the lions if only to escape from the roar of the traffic which is continuous. (There are six main roads into, and out of, the square which functions on the one-way roundabout system with an inner lane on the west side for taxis and buses only.) Exploring the statues is a rather dull business. There are bronze busts of Admirals Beatty and Jellicoe of the First World War, and Cunningham of the Second, on the north wall, at the east end of which is George IV on horseback high on a plinth, unmatched by a similar figure at the opposite end. On the north wall, also, are the Imperial Standards of Length carved into the stone. They were cut in 1976. By reference to them you may settle arguments about the exact measurement of an imperial yard, chain, pole or perch. On the south side of the square, as we leave to take the zebra to Charing Cross, as the highway, here several unmarked lanes wide, is still named, we pass the statue of a general who, with any luck, will have a pigeon, deadpan mockery in its eyes, perched on his head. And that is not *all* the general will suffer. (The pigeon, of course, is real; the zebra is the name given to a pedestrian crossing.)

Once over the road we leave the square (there will be more to say about both the National Gallery and St Martin's in future walks) and make for Admiralty Arch which, with the Mall beyond it, commemorates Queen Victoria and not Nelson. It is really a screen with five arches, one for ceremonial processions when the wrought-iron gates are opened, two for everyday traffic and two for pedestrians. Above and beside the arches of this rather ponderous structure are offices belonging to the Admiralty, the mass of which is in and behind nearby Whitehall.

Cross to the left side of the Mall which, at weekends, is pedestrianized for most of its length. Close to the office of the Privy Council (a body of some three hundred persons, mostly present or past ministers of the crown, whose duties, except upon the death of a monarch, are minimal) is a statue to Captain Cook, and just beyond it a sandy-coloured edifice smothered in creeper. This, the Citadel, looks like the type of desert fort you expect to see besieged by foreign legionnaires. In fact, it is an air raid shelter built during the Second World War for government use. According to David Piper it has an acre of grass on its roof.

St James's Park looks inviting and is, and will remain beside us all the way along the Mall, but it is too soon to take a rest. Instead, note the lamp standards with their marine motif of a boat surmounting twin lights, in honour of the nearby Admiralty. Then take in the splendid view towards Buck House, as those who are never likely to be invited to a levée there familiarly call it, and cross to Carlton House Terrace, above which looms another martial figure atop another column. It is the grand Old Duke of York, the one alluded to in the popular song, who marched his ten thousand men to the top of

The Grand Old Duke of York Waterloo Place

the hill in order to march them down again. He was the son of George III and commander-in-chief during a period of army reform. Those of his ten thousand still serving at his death lost a day's pay each to subscribe to his monument, which is well sited at the top of wide steps leading into Waterloo Place.

Walk up the Mall until you are opposite the Duke's column in order to take in the scale of Nash's two elegant terraces which replaced a royal residence called Carlton House. Remember that you are looking at the back of them (we shall see the fronts on Walk Eight), but what other buildings have such handsome posteriors? On each, above what would now be called the garden floor (some garden!) is a balustrade with more than twenty pillars reaching up to the third floor, above which is a pediment amongst attic windows. Where the pillars cease at each end of the building are wings five bays wide carried squarely to above the attic level with eye windows set back between shorter columns. Into the lower part of the eastern terrace a gallery for the Institute of Contemporary Arts has been incorporated without spoiling Nash's design.

Standing above the next steps which come down from Carlton Gardens is a stone statue of George VI dressed as an admiral of the fleet. He was king during World War Two and took pride in being resident in his palace during the blitz. Near by is the rear of Marlborough House where his mother, Queen Mary, lived during her widowhood. This house, and St James's Palace, we view from the front in a later walk. Between the latter and Lancaster House, where important conferences are held, such as those attended by heads of the Commonwealth, is Stable Yard Road which gives an impression of forbidden territory. Many thoroughfares in London do, but everyone uses them.

Now it is time to concentrate on Buckingham Palace, about which one should adopt a theatrical approach, viewing it as the setting for a prodigiously successful and long-running pageant play, for the most part immaculately acted by the Queen and her family, plus her 'hosts of hangers-on'. Our twentieth-century version of monarchy, a far cry from that lengthy line of murderers, double-dealers, lunatics and playboys who held the throne – often tenuously – for most of our recorded history, has survived into an age when most other crowned heads of Europe have either rolled or been roughly cast aside. It has done so not in the gently democratic, bicycle-riding manner of the Dutch and Scandinavian kings and queens, but by adapting to the fine theatrical traditions of the country which have never been confined to the playhouse and the screen. They have entered into court and parliamentary procedure, which often emphasizes the national brilliance for wearing outlandish costume and enduring rituals of amazing subtlety and/or silliness. These are carried out with such conviction that giggles are stifled, superior smiles freeze on the lips and there is scarcely a dry eye all the way from the Palace to St Paul's. Anyone who saw the televising of the marriage ceremony of the Prince and Princess of Wales in 1981 (and it is questionable whether, outside the Gulag Archipelago, anyone did not) will know this, which is why I say you must approach Buckingham Palace as though you expect the curtain to rise at any moment.

If you advance on it whilst the Mall is free from traffic you may safely pause in the middle of that wide avenue. On one side is a pillar with the words W AFRICA engraved on it; on the other is its twin S AFRICA. These were not partners in some prosperous legal practice but member colonies of an empire which has evolved into independent states. Between them, across one arc of what is popularly known as a roundabout, is the memorial to Queen Victoria, the monarch who made royalty respectable just in time despite guerrilla activity from some of her offspring, notably the womanizing son who succeeded her, Edward VII. She gave her name to an era perhaps simply because she came to the throne so young and remained on it for so long. Now her statue sits high on a grotesquely ornate assemblage with a winged victory and other figures in gold leaf flouncing about above her. In deference to Prince Albert, to whom she was married for twenty-one of the sixty-four years of her reign,

Buckingham Palace

she wears a wedding ring on her right hand. Albert was a German and that was, and is, the custom in his country. Their grandchildren included the last royal ruler of Germany, Wilhelm II (Kaiser Bill) and the Princess who married Nicholas, Tsar of all the Russias, and perished with him after the communist revolution.

In recent years Victoria has ceased to be a figure of fun to the literary *cognoscenti*. Lytton Strachey's debunking assessment of her has given way to an understanding of her prowess as diarist, painter and constitutional monarch. Etiquette at her court was almost as rigid as at Versailles and would be found intolerable today, but she also knew about pageantry, so it is appropriate that she should stand, in all her marble glory, before the palace which she made her home, and which was enlarged to accommodate her family.

The Edwardian east façade which closes the three-sided courtyard created by Nash is the backdrop to our scene, across which figures move, some in military dress, others in formal morning attire hurrying to appointments connected with the household business of the palace, or to receive medals making them members or companions of an order of the empire upon which the sun set finally many years ago. In the foreground a chorus of sightseers crowd about the railings, hoping to glimpse a royal personage.

As the time approaches for the weekly, or at some periods fortnightly, changing of the guard, or the daily mounting of the same, the crowd swells to Cecil B. De Mille proportions. A state carriage may be driven in or out, and, on very special occasions, the Queen and her family and distinguished visitors may appear on the balcony under the central pediment, and wave. No one will be much interested in the wave of a visitor, although polite applause will greet it. It is the *royal British wave* which matters, and this is given and accepted in an underplayed cameo reflecting the modern naturalistic style of acting. It is none the less effective for that.

At up-market events, such as coronations and royal weddings, Cinderella coaches come into play and there is pomp and glitter as the procession sweeps around the back of Victoria and the figures way below her feet. Two of them were presented by New Zealand, one representing agriculture as a woman with a sickle, the other industry, as a man wielding a massive hammer. Hammer and sickle. Very droll.

The Palace originated in humbler shape, as Buckingham House, home of the Duke of that name in the very early eighteenth century. When he arrived Arlington House occupied a site approximating to the grander house which he ordered to be erected. William Winde was commissioned to design something better situated to take in the

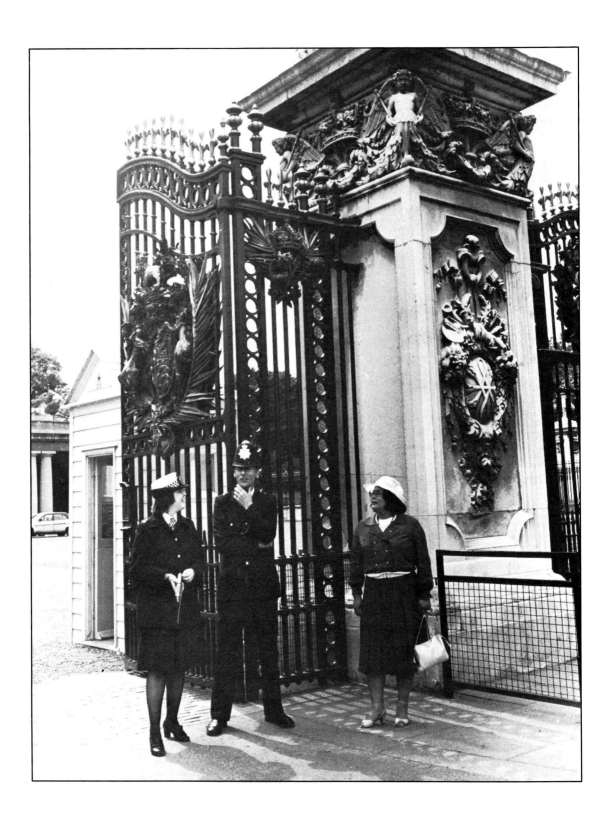

view of the Mall which Charles II had laid out with four lines of trees. It was this Buckingham House which became a royal residence in 1762 when George III and Queen Charlotte found they preferred it to Kensington and to St James's Palace. (The latter was retained for official functions.)

George IV, who lived at Carlton House, had Nash design the present palace (the expense of which again upset Parliament) within the shell of the Duke's house, but he did not live to enjoy it. Nor did his successor William IV, who reigned for only seven years. During Victoria's long tenure there were major alterations. The Marble Arch which Nash placed in the open courtyard between the north and south wings was removed to allow for the new east front, and sent off to stand alone near Speakers' Corner at the north-east edge of Hyde Park. This frontage was rebuilt by Sir Aston Webb, in Portland stone, shortly before World War One. Since then there have been no significant changes to the structure, which was only slightly damaged by bombs in the Second War, the main casualty being the chapel which is now the Queen's Gallery. Pevsner tells us that to understand the architecture of B. P., Nash's design of the west front needs to be seen. Unless you are one of the nine thousand guests invited to a royal garden party (nine thousand handshakes!) or you become a personal friend of the family – which is possible – you are unlikely to enjoy this experience. The palace is not open to casual visitors and most of us must be content with appreciating it vicariously from the photographs and descriptions published in books. The small Pitkin publication has excellent colour photographs of richly decorated halls, staircases, ceilings, galleries and chambers, and an aerial view of the site showing the extensive lawn, with a lake beyond it, where garden parties are held.

When you have given up hope of seeing a princess in a glass coach pass by, leave, not by Constitution Hill, but by Buckingham Gate, where you will find the entrances to both the Queen's Gallery and the Royal Mews. The former is open weekdays (except Mondays), 11–5; Sundays 2–5. It is approached along an enclosed passage hung with drawings and photographs of royalty in action. There are even cartoons which make fun of them – copies should be sent to all members of the Politburo and to Third World leaders.

The actual gallery, rebuilt from the ruins of the chapel in 1961, is tall and almost square with steep steps up and down from a double-L-shaped balcony. There is no permanent exhibition but those mounted run for twelve to fifteen months and comprise items from the royal collection, which is spread over several palaces, houses, and castles. There is a charge for admission.

Police and Tourist
Buckingham Palace
(opposite)

The Royal Mews, further along Buckingham Gate, is open only on Wednesdays and Thursdays (2–4). You must pay for that also. How many more would pay for entrance into the Palace proper? Considering the rate of inflation, it is by no means unlikely that this is being thought about seriously.

The opposite side of Buckingham Gate has handsome houses, especially No. 2, which was built as a hotel in the 1860s. It has seven bays each side of a wide front door and rises to five storeys plus an attic where the Victorian maids presumably shared mean bedrooms. (What whited sepulchres opulent buildings so often are with their squalid basements and fire-trap roof rooms.) The last use of No. 2 was as offices for the British Airports Authority.

We turn right at Lower Grosvenor Place, still following the walls which enclose the palace and its grounds. Ahead there is a glimpse of the Grosvenor Hotel which stands beside Victoria Station, 'The Gateway to the Continent'. Here the famed Orient Express began its journeys to Istanbul. (The revived service goes only to Venice.)

On the corner of Victoria Square is a delightful building with what Pevsner calls 'domed rounded corners', but how can a corner be round? It is at the end of a terrace leading into what would be a secluded square if there weren't so many recent towerblocks overpowering it. In it at No. 8 is a plaque to the Scottish poet Thomas Campbell. On another cofner of Lower Grosvenor Place is a pub called the Bag O'Nails. A minor joy of walking London is collecting curious inn signs and names.

The back garden wall of the Palace (you can see over it from the top of a bus) stretches away up Grosvenor Place to Hyde Park Corner but we cross into Hobart Place, noting the solid blocks in Grosvenor Gardens, lying obliquely away from us. They have pavilion roofs in the French style and are part of the estate developed by the Cundys, father and son. Cundy senior was surveyor of Lord Grosvenor's estate, spreading over the area now known as Belgravia, which we are about to enter, and far beyond. The second Earl Grosvenor was Viscount Belgrave until the death of his father and was later created the first Marquis of Westminster. It was he who employed Thomas Cubitt to build the squares and crescents on partly marshy ground to the west of Buckingham Palace. Cubitt had already been involved in the extension of the Bedford estate in Bloomsbury and was also at work on St Katharine's Dock by the Tower. From the latter site he transported earth to swampy Belgravia, which was to become a fashionable district of London – and not accidentally, for its development coincided with the transformation of Buckingham House into Buckingham Palace.

At the end of Hobart Place we enter Eaton Square which is only partly Cubitt's work. He had a finger in so many pies that, man of prodigious energy though he was, he had to delegate and sub-contract. So the north of the square is his, the south is by W. H. Seth-Smith and the church of St Peter's, placed at one end and looking very much like an afterthought, is by Henry Hakewill, with additions by Sir Arthur Blomfield.

Eaton Square, which is rectangular, is spoilt by the King's Road which runs down the centre and two others which cross it. The terraces on all sides are thus interrupted but this was intentional because Eaton Square was part of an overall plan including Belgrave Square to the north and Chester Square to the south. They are fine terraces with much variation of detail. Some have stone balustrades, some iron balconies. One has a colonnade at ground- and first-floor levels, others have separate portals or columns on varying storeys. The general effect is gracious and, in literary terms, Jamesian. Two

Embassy territory
Eaton Square

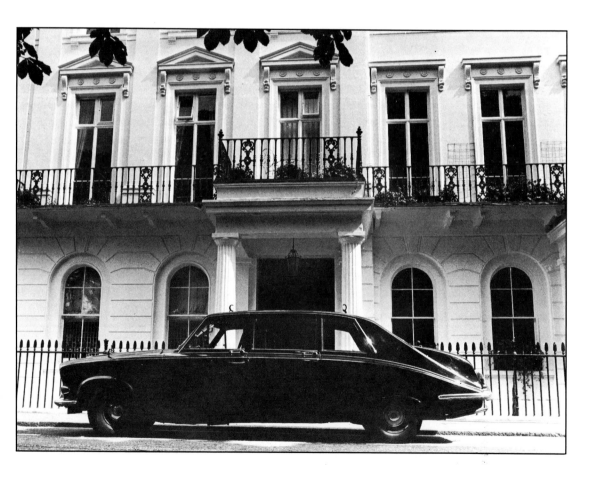

conservative prime ministers – Stanley Baldwin and Neville Chamberlain – lived here. So, for a few months in 1848, did Prince Metternich when he fled the revolution in Vienna. A fourth plaque records that, at No. 80, George Peabody, the American whose statue we saw behind the Royal Exchange on Walk One, died in 1869. We shall come across the Peabody Buildings which the millionaire built to improve the housing conditions of the poor more than once on our walks. Designs for workers' flats have improved since 1869, although not in all cases. Paradoxically some of those built for Peabody have been converted into desirable bijou one-person apartments.

Having arrived at Eaton Square we leave it at once, turning right at St Peter's church into Upper Belgrave Street which leads into Belgrave Square. This square is octagonal and we take it anticlockwise, noting as we enter a statue on the edge of the gardens to Simón Bolívar, the Latin-American soldier who with British help freed his native Venezuela and neighbouring states from Spanish rule. He faces away from the Spanish Embassy whose utterly charming house we pass as we leave the Square. Belgravia is much associated with diplomacy, and evidence of it is marked here at its heart. In contrast to Eaton Square, although it has as many traffic arteries entering it, the effect is quite different because none of them bisects it. So the central area of green, where on a warm June afternoon I saw not a soul in the private gardens or using the tennis courts, allows that sense of serenity, so endemic to the squares of London, to permeate the atmosphere.

Belgrave is a connoisseur's square and the final exquisite touch comes as you leave it to return to Eaton Square. There on the diagonal joining Chesham Place to Belgrave Place is the Spanish Embassy, a gem of a residence, not too large to be ostentatious, not so small as to infringe the dignity of a Don. It stands back a little way from the road behind a small, railinged garden, three storeys high in the centre, two at its symmetrical sides. A columned portico gives it importance without pomposity; a street vendor selling flowers adds humanity.

When we reach Eaton Square again the Belgian Embassy on our left provides less cause for rhapsody, being just a part of one of Cubitt's handsome terraces. (Oh, lucky diplomats who inhabit it.)

Walk along the terrace on your right until you come to Eaton Place, then go left to Eaton Gate where you turn right for Sloane Square. This will give you an opportunity of admiring two of the terraces at close quarters.

Once out of Eaton Square and into Cliveden Place at a point where the King's Road ceases for a while, you are on the actual grazing grounds of the Sloane Ranger, SW3's answer to Hampstead Man.

In Sloane Square is the Royal Court Theatre, and a hotel and tavern of the same name. The Theatre is important for two periods during which it exercised far-reaching influence on the English drama. The first was from 1904 to 1907 when the Vedrenne/Granville-Barker management staged new plays by Shaw, Galsworthy and Barker himself, as well as carefully produced revivals especially of the Greek classics. It was very badly damaged by bombs in 1941 and did not reopen until the early 1950s. In 1956 the English Stage Company was inaugurated under George Devine and its third production was John Osborne's *Look Back in Anger* which changed the course of modern English playwriting. The ESC has remained loyal to the new school of dramatists but has also specialized in plays by contemporary continental writers. It was here that Olivier appeared in one of his greatest roles, Archie Rice in *The Entertainer*. The Royal

Sloane Square

Court also has a studio for experimental plays called The Theatre Upstairs.

The Square is the gateway to Chelsea which is outside my terms of reference and has an ever-growing literature of its own. The King's Road, which resumes its course by the Peter Jones department store at the south-west entrance, is the birthplace of all that is trendy; we go north into Sloane Street which is long and straight, and much less glittering. At the beginning is a beast of a church (Holy Trinity), a fat lump of a building with four spires which look like candles that have got out of hand. Pevsner says it is 'the outstanding London example of the Arts and Craft Movement in the ecclesiastical field'. Alastair Service in his *Architects of London* calls it 'a major Arts and Crafts Gothic work'. More to my taste are two striking blocks of flats (late Victorian?) on either side of Wilbraham Place opposite. They are red brick with white plaster windows, frames and woodwork. They are four bays wide and long, and four storeys high with shops at ground level: most pleasing and simple compositions.

The street continually excites attention. There is an elegant shop with intricately structured chandeliers twinkling above antique furniture and, soon after on the same side, lying back and beside a sunken garden with tennis courts, Cadogan Place. It is correct to call it Chelsea rather than Belgravia because it comes within that Royal Borough, not the City of Westminster, but I daresay some who live there in the mostly nineteenth-century houses, all sprucely maintained, prefer Belgravia. It doesn't matter. The fourth side of the Place is still Sloane Street with pleasing apartment blocks in brick, a description which does not apply to the hideous Danish Embassy, sick in colour and conception, with a heavy blast wall at pavement level. The latter, alas, was probably born of necessity through terrorism. Next to it stands a slim mock-Tudor house with fussy windows and bays, and a mass of superfluous decoration. It is in pleasing contrast to its paranoid neighbour.

There are plaques to Sir Charles Dilke, the Liberal politician whose career ended abruptly when he was found to be having an affair with a lady who was not his wife, and to Sir Herbert Beerbohm-Tree, the actor-manager who was the first Henry Higgins in *Pygmalion*. It was he who, when asked by a young actress for help in interpreting a role, replied, 'I want you to speak it in a *mauve* voice.'

Near the end of Cadogan Place, Pont Street crosses it, which gives an opportunity of identifying what Osbert Lancaster defined as Pont Street Dutch, thus establishing the credentials of an architectural style. When you observe the details you will see what he meant, his wit being just a part of his scholarship.

At the north end of the street are shopping parades on either side with hotels looming above them. The shops have names such as Please Mum, Young Motherhood, La Cicogna and, more down to earth, Truslove & Hanson, a bookshop of fine pedigree. At the top on the right is Harvey Nichols, a store which you might think imposing until you turn left and react to the huge red hulk which is Harrods. Dominating both, and much else, is the Bowater Building, a glass monster with flags of all nations flying above it. The traffic, on its way to Hyde Park, passes beneath it through Edinburgh Gate.

Harrods
Selecting the Correct
Shade of Dark Grey

Make for Harrods, a terracotta baroque and Byzantine fantasy with domes and pinnacles and the royal coat of arms emblazoned on it. This is the crowned head of all department stores. A friend of mine once wrote, 'If the rest of London were to be submerged Harrods could manage on its own for a while.' It may or may not be the largest department store in Britain, Europe, or the world, but it is the most prestigious. It is formidably individual although it has long been part of a group and is frequently the subject of takeover rumours. Its business is in quality whatever the product and it claims to be able to supply everything from a ranch to a greetings card. It has customers in most parts of the world; it also has its own style of clientèle at the thought of which some other traders blench. In my Hampstead bookshop, if anyone is especially truculent and demanding, we always say he or, more probably, she, has escaped from Harrods. But the best as well as the worst are attracted to Knightsbridge to this great bazaar, this high temple of the consumer society. Stores have little appeal to me. They are always overheated and crowded and daylight is not allowed to penetrate far inside them, but if I had to use one it would be Harrods. If I lived in this part of London I would regularly succumb to the allure of its marbled food halls, even, perhaps, to its Boulangerie, the like of which I have never encountered in your actual France.

Harrods' address is Knightsbridge but it is really in Brompton Road, a thoroughfare which exudes good taste through its many expertly dressed shop windows. You must cross it at some point on your way to Museumland and you should do so before the junction with Brompton Square, which is neither rectangle nor octagon, but an inverted U. It dates from the 1820s and whatever damage it suffered in the Second World War has been carefully rectified. Not at all 'period' are the many burglar-alarm devices on the houses, signifying an area of high risk for insurance. On No. 6 is a plaque to the French poet, Stéphane Mallarmé, who lived here in 1863, having come to London to learn English. He stayed to marry a German governess and taught our language for the rest of his poverty-stricken life.

We join Cromwell Road at the Brompton Oratory of St Philip Neri, a baroque Roman Catholic church in which there is a wax model of the saint lying as a relic in a coffin with transparent covering. Everything in the interior is mud-coloured except for pairs of burgundy red panels. The acoustics are perfect, so that many recordings have been made here. There is a splendid dome and the statuary from Siena adds to the intended impression of being in an Italian cathedral, which one would not automatically have guessed from the name of the architect, Herbert Gribble. Outside in a niche is a statue to Cardinal Newman whose defection to Roman Catholicism rocked ecclesiastical England in mid-Victorian times.

Here now is Museumland, the Albertian corner of London celebrating Victoria's consort who died in his prime ten years after the Great Exhibition of 1851 was held in Hyde Park. He was the basic inspiration for all we are about to see. The monument erected to him represented collective identification with the Queen's grief. First we see the Victoria and Albert Museum, to appreciate which it is necessary to cross the wide road to Thurloe Place.

It is a combination of cathedral, palace and railway station with a very busy skyline crowned by a figure with a halo who is Christ, not Albert. It embraces many architectural styles with a Grecian centrepiece, one octagonal tower upon another, both liberally colonnaded beneath an open cupola, above a renaissance church entrance. Sir Aston Webb was the principal architect; he had a ball.

The V&A, as it is popularly known, houses a huge collection which so thorough a reference book as the Blue Guide *Museums and Galleries of London* does not pretend to list comprehensively. Even so it devotes eighteen closely-printed pages to describing the cream of what is to be found in its, approximately, 150 rooms. It was founded, on the initiative of Prince Albert, as the Museum of Manufactures and became part of the South Kensington Museum in 1857. Its object, allied to the Prince's championing of the Great Exhibition, was to encourage development of British decorative design by showing examples of ancient and contemporary work. The collection is on several floors and mezzanines displaying paintings, prints, ceramics, furniture, sculpture, glass, tapestries, carpets, tiles, ivories, musical instruments, shop fronts, ceilings, wallpapers, textiles, altarpieces, silverware, candlesticks, costumes, clocks, locks, cutlery and much else besides. The Great Bed of Ware (late sixteenth-century), measuring 12 feet by 12 feet, is here – so is William Morris's Green Dining-Room which he designed with Philip Webb. There is an Adam ceiling from David Garrick's house at 6, Adelphi Terrace, and seven of the ten cartoons which Raphael produced as designs for tapestries now in the Vatican. Once I heard a woman, outraged, exclaim, 'Cartoons, they call them! I can't see what's funny.' Today their subjects, taken from the Acts of the Apostles, might easily inspire a cartoonist to satirical comment.

In 1983 the Henry Cole wing of the V&A was opened. It is joined to the main museum but can be entered separately from Exhibition Road. I would recommend reaching it by an interior route if only because, almost at the linking point, is one of the most engaging exhibits in the entire museum – Canova's sculpture *A Sleeping Nymph*. Can you resist patting her marbled buttocks? I can't.

Sir Henry Cole was Secretary of the Department of Science and Art and put into practice Prince Albert's vision of the Museum. The wing now named after him was formerly part of the Imperial College of Science but has been converted to house the V&A's collection of prints, photographs and paintings. On the top floor is a gallery almost exclusively devoted to John Constable whose work is displayed in an ambience of entirely appropriate serenity. Here are his canvases of Hampstead Heath and Salisbury Cathedral, the Academy pictures in elaborate gilt frames, the others simply mounted. It is the final outpost of the Museum – only those who really care about the painter are likely to find it. There are lifts but I recommend the stairs, where one can stop at each level to examine the early photographs and fine watercolours, the old masters and the panorama of Rome. On the staircases are life-size mosaics of great Italian painters done by Watts and other Victorian artists.

Another, perhaps temporary, feature is the Boilerhouse Project which is completely in the spirit of Prince Albert's original conception for 'museumland'. It is the inspiration of the Conran Foundation and its object is to 'provide stimulus for students, designers and for manufacturing industry'. It is here at the V&A, literally in the old boilerhouse yard of the museum, on a short lease, while premises are found for a permanent home. It ought to remain because it is very relevant to the original purpose not only of the V&A but of the whole complex of museums which we are visiting.

The V&A also houses the National Art Library which may be used by casual visitors on signature of the Visitors' Book, but regular users must have letters of introduction from some learned person or body. The opening hours are the same as for the museum – weekdays, except Fridays, 10–5.50; Sundays 2.30–5.50, but times are subject to alteration and some museum rooms have more restricted opening times. Entry is free, as it is to most national collections. The principle is good but I believe there is a strong argument for charging admission provided that funds go directly to the galleries and museums and not to the Treasury. Students, OAPs, the unemployed and children under a certain age could be allowed in free; as could children between 8 and 18 on production of a certificate of good behaviour by a head teacher.

It is a pity that our ancient puritanical laws, bolstered up by such ludicrous organizations as the Lord's Day Observance Society, and certain trade unions, do not permit the museums to open on Sunday mornings when there is extensive demand for them. Witness the long queues which form outside most museums before the Sunday afternoon opening time.

Across Exhibition Road from the V&A is the Natural History Museum; up Exhibition Road are the Geological and Science Museums. The Nat. Hist. is another cathedral-style edifice but in Romanesque, by Alfred Waterhouse, who used terracotta in pale ochre and blue (at least these are the colours now). It is a department of the British Museum and originated in a lifelong collection made by Sir Hans Sloane, a distinguished physician (1660–1753) whose name is preserved in the square and street we have visited, and also in Hans Crescent, Place and Road beside and behind Harrods. He was one-time title-holder to the Manor of Chelsea and bequeathed his collection to the nation on payment of £20,000 to his family. He had spent more than £50,000 in amassing it. The Museum, which has had many extensions since the Waterhouse building was erected, some

Natural History Museum

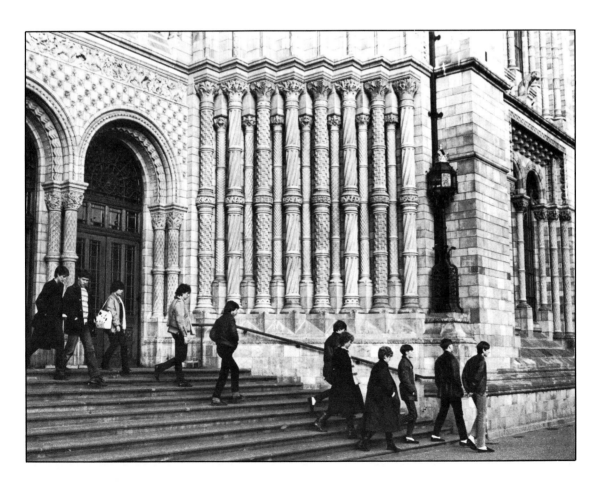

more attractive than others, has sections for Birds, Plants, Butterflies, Mammals, Minerals, Rocks and Gemstones, Insects and so on.

Once inside the sense of visiting a cathedral gives way to a strong hunch that one is in a Victorian Gothic railway station and that the dinosaur now standing at platform 1 will pound off almost immediately. It is an arrestingly dramatic presentation. The reconstructed skeleton of the ancient creature can be viewed from various levels, and should be. The mostly young visitors to the museum emphasize this. They busily ascend and descend the great staircase, parading through the various galleries making awesome noises, but reserving most of their attention for the dinosaur. The blue whale is almost an anti-climax, yet it should be seen, as should much else relating to birds, beasts, fish and insects. There is almost too much. The museum is open all weekdays 10–6; Sundays 2.30–6.

Turn left as you leave the Museum, then left again into Exhibition Road. The Geological Museum comes first and it is a poor relation of the others because it is not as popular, but this means it is likely to be less crowded which has advantages. You can see the Koh-i-noor diamond and a piece of moon rock brought back by Apollo 16. It has an earthquake simulator for those who like to live dangerously, and, behind suitable protection, radioactive minerals. It also shows a film about the world's first thousand million years, and another about the last six hundred million (last meaning latest). And there is a globe which spins on its axis. In the upper galleries there are reference sections which are of great value to scholars but not of much interest to the casual visitor. The whole message of the museum seems to be to convey how short a time man has been a dominant factor in the universe. Perhaps one should visit it often to maintain a proper humility.

Next door is the Science Museum (weekdays 10–6; Sundays 2.30–6, the same as for the Geological) another institution calculated to make me feel not one, but many, down. I can think of no other building which displays so much that is beyond my comprehension. Attempting to describe it, I recall the misery I experienced when as a cub reporter I was sent on to the Downs above Eastbourne to watch a new combine harvester being demonstrated. The story I filed about it was one of the shortest ever printed.

However, there are exhibits in the Science Museum which are not totally beyond my ken and I appreciate the imaginative way in which it is laid out. There is Puffing Billy, the oldest locomotive in the world, and numerous examples of railway rolling stock. There are bicycles, motorcars, aircraft and ships; tramcars, ploughs and tractors. Just inside the entrance hall is Foucault's Pendulum showing how the earth rotates on its own axis, and there are engines, engines everywhere – beam engines, triple-expansion steam engines, atmospheric, oil and turbine engines, mostly on the ground floor. Up above there are galleries devoted to chemistry, physics, printing, aeronautics, photography, telecommunications and one thousand and one items of technology and science illustrating man's subtlety and inventiveness. There is a gallery for children which, says David Piper in his *Illustrated Companion Guide to London* 'is one of the dottiest, most pleasurable places'. Here you can try to grab a floating golden ball, interrupt a photo-electric cell to pass through a door, operate burglar alarms and miniature crane grabs. (So you see what I mean about that Certificate of Good Behaviour.) Old, as well as young, are attracted to the gallery on space exploration which has a replica of the Sea of Tranquillity and a sign saying PLEASE KEEP OFF THE MOON.

The Museum occupies five levels, including a lower ground floor. It was founded in 1856 and moved into the present building in 1928. The amenities include a small theatre where instructional films are shown and lectures given, a tea-room and a children's lunch-room. On the top floor is the Wellcome Museum of the History of Medicine.

On leaving, walk up Exhibition Road as far as Prince Consort Road and turn left into it past the City and Guilds Engineering College, to the Royal College of Music. This faces the Albert Hall, a late-Victorian amphitheatre which houses a variety of entertainments from symphony concerts to boxing contests, regimental reunions, political rallies and carol services. It was once the venue for the Chelsea Arts Ball until that event had to be abandoned because of what was then thought to be the permissive behaviour of those supporting it. It stands in Kensington Gore, its circularity (Piper says it is really oval) broken by the entrance portals facing Kensington Gardens. A cloister runs all round the building and provides resting-space on many weary nights for those who queue for tickets for the Last Night of the Proms, a popular national festival which is televised. The Promenade Concerts were started in 1895 by Sir Henry Wood who conducted them annually in the Queen's Hall (near Oxford Circus) until it was blitzed. Since then, under the auspices of the BBC, they have taken place at the Albert Hall although some events, usually choral, are occasionally performed elsewhere. At one time, before the invention of broadcasting, the Proms provided the only opportunity that many people had of listening to serious music and of getting to know the classical repertory at little expense. The cheapest admittance is to the central floor where there are no seats, and you 'promenade', or to the upper galleries where you can lie on the floor and listen

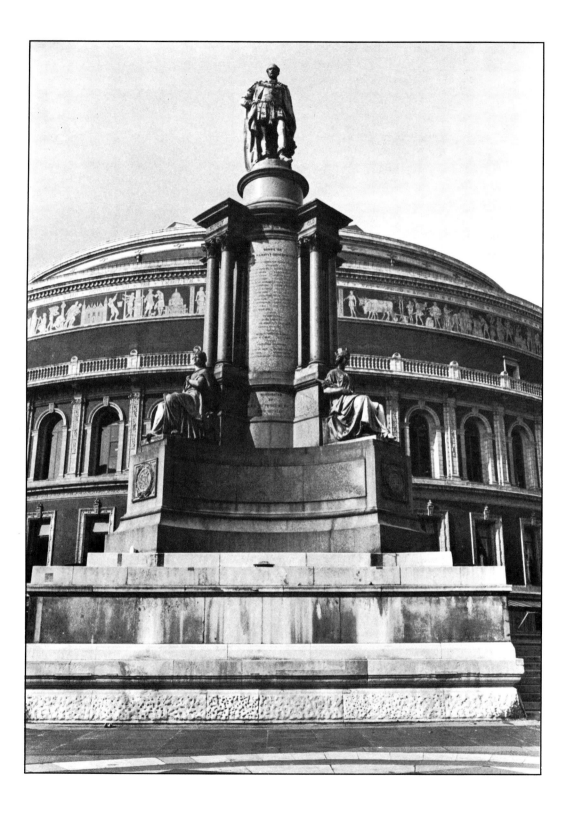

without seeing. Nowadays the programmes are less traditionally planned and it is not possible to hear all the symphonies of Schubert and Dvořák, say, in one season, but instead there are the Royal Festival Hall, the Barbican Hall and Radio Three, not to mention discs and cassettes. The final Friday of the season, however, is still reserved for Beethoven's Choral Symphony, and woe betide the conductor who seeks to vary too much the programme for the last night when Henry Wood's arrangement of sea shanties is sung, when streamers and balloons are thrown from the balconies and fancy dress is worn by the promenaders who have, amazingly, kept awake. Until recently the proceedings regularly ended with 'Rule Britannia' and 'Land of Hope and Glory' but the former is thought not to be quite appropriate any more, which is a pity. Never mind the words. It is a splendid tune and a powerful contralto was always brought sweeping on, tiara twinkling, to pitch herself against the Hall's famous echo, an acoustical problem which the management now believes it has solved.

The arena is at several levels with private boxes which can be hired from their owners, on two of them, and seats beside and behind the performers except where the mighty organ with its approximately 9,000 pipes takes up the space. The boxes were sold (£1,000 each on the first tier, £500 on the second) to defray the cost of the building, which was about £200,000, a huge sum for 1871.

In the offices and rooms off the top corridors the Central School of Speech and Drama was once housed. Among the many now famous actors and actresses who studied there are Laurence Olivier and Peggy Ashcroft who shared the gold medal in one vintage year. Performances were given in a theatre built into the curve of the building, between the outside wall and the arena. Stage and auditorium were thus also curved but less sharply than in a classical theatre and with far less depth. There were only, memory tells me, three rows of seats, but the theatre is no longer there.

On the outside of the Albert Hall a frieze concerned with the Triumph of Arts and Letters runs all the way round and notes that Queen Victoria opened it. (She was a busy lady in these parts.) The Hall can accommodate eight thousand people. Beside it stands the Royal College of Organists, with a frieze of cherubic musicians, some clothed in flowing robes, some naked, and opposite is the Albert Memorial, as preposterous a monument as you will find anywhere in the capital, although it is becoming fashionable to admire it. It is by Sir George Gilbert Scott (that's how he got his knighthood) and features poor Albert seated within an open-sided square temple, crowded with ornamentation. It has spires, pinnacles, statues, a cross on the top and is flanked by groups in marble above sculpted friezes

The Royal Albert Hall and Prince Albert's lesser-known memorial (opposite)

on the plinth. These are worth examining in detail. At the front, facing the Albert Hall, sits Homer playing his lyre. On his left is Shakespeare with ear cupped as though he can't quite catch the music. Dante, on his right, looks up adoringly. The east side group has Raphael in the central position, with Michelangelo on his left, leaning slightly forward with a puzzled expression, as much as to say, 'why am I not in the middle?' His right arm has a proprietorial hold on Raphael's chair. On the other side Leonardo looks away pensively. Giotto is in this group and in another on the north side. There are also soldiers, sailors, scientists, statesmen, great men and women of all nations.

Service calls the Memorial 'a concentrated example of the best mid-Victorian craftsmanship'; Pevsner says it is 'rich, solid, and a little pompous, a little vulgar, but full of faith and self-confidence'. The first illustrated cover of *Private Eye* showed it, as it is, with the caption 'Albert Gristle Awaits Blast-Off'. I can never see it without being reminded of that irreverent comment.

There is one more building to visit before we rest in Hyde Park. This is Kensington Palace, a few minutes away, along the Flower and Broad Walks and beside the Round Pond (which is not round). By continental standards it is a small villa, the sort of place a Habsburg might have given to a favourite old retainer for his retirement, but it was good enough for William and Mary who came jointly to the throne of Britain when the Roman Catholic James II thought it prudent to leave the country. William suffered from asthma and wished to live well away from London, at Hampton Court, Henry VIII's palace where Christopher Wren (who enlarged it) died. His advisers protested that he must reside nearer to Whitehall. Mary fell for what was then Nottingham House and soon had Wren and others working to transform it into a modest palace where, only six years later, she died of smallpox, followed, after another eight, by William. His successor, Queen Anne, also died there, as did the second of the Hanoverians who inherited the throne through descent from Charles I. This might have seemed a dubious claim but did not matter because constitutional monarchy was ready to put paid to the divine right of kings and the madness of George III accelerated the process. The latter cannot be blamed for not wishing to live in the little palace where so many of his predecessors had ended their days, and went, as we have seen, to Buckingham House. Kensington became a monarch's residence again only temporarily when the young Princess Victoria, who was born there, became Queen on the death of her uncle William IV. After Victoria's removal to Buckingham Palace, Kensington became the home of the Tecks, whose daughter, Princess Mary,

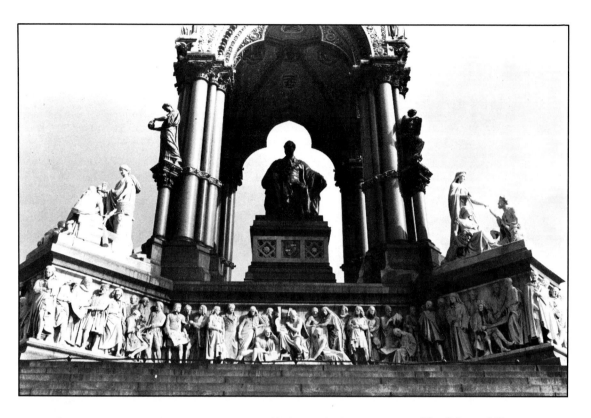

married Victoria's grandson George, grandfather of the present Queen.

The 'Homer' Frieze on the Albert Memorial

Let that be an end of genealogy which is a tiresome subject. The palace was bombed in the Second World War and, when restored, hosted the London Museum which, as we know, was later amalgamated with the Guildhall Museum, in the City, to become the Museum of London. The rooms thus vacated are to become a centre for the Court Dress Collection. Others are already open to the public from 10 on weekdays, and 2 p.m. on Sundays. There is a charge for admission. Among the chambers open are the King's Gallery with a decorated ceiling by William Kent; the Presence Chamber, built by Wren (it now has the most ill-matching wallpaper and painted ceiling); and the Cupola Room with marble ionic columns at its entrance. Here Princess Victoria was christened but only after a lengthy argument between the Prince Regent (deputising for the temporarily deranged King George III) and the Duke of Kent, the baby's father. While they wrangled about what the princess should be named, the Archbishop of Canterbury waited, dangling the child over the, presumably, improvised font. Other rooms which may be seen are Victoria's bedroom and the Queen's Gallery (by Wren) in which

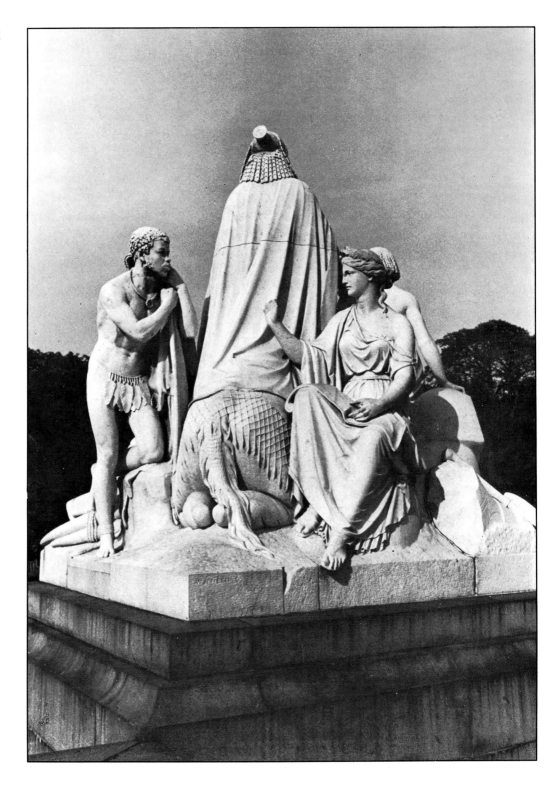

there are portraits of those childless monarchs, William and Mary. She is shown as a handsome, ample-bosomed young lady of 23; he looks every inch a Stuart, which he was, as well as being an Orange.

From the Privy Chamber you can see the courtyard and pretty clock tower; from windows on the other side, the garden, with trees trained to make covered walks, is visible. There is much in the Palace to interest the lover of Victoriana and earlier bric-à-brac, including a statue of Lady Godiva, given by Victoria to Albert as a birthday present. This was surely very daring of her but presumably she understood his tastes.

Following your visit walk back into Kensington Gardens towards the Long Water, the thin extension of the Serpentine which is Hyde Park's Lake. A statue of Peter Pan stands there. It is by George Frampton and celebrates the character which J. M. Barrie created first for *The Little White Bird*, a story set in Kensington Gardens, and then immortalized in the play which is still performed annually in London. The model for the statue was Nina Boucicault, the actress who created Peter, who here stands on a muddy brown rock playing a pipe. Very English looking lady angels swirl about beneath him amongst bronze mice and rabbits. At this spot Peter was supposed to have landed his boats. After so much fact let us indulge this fantasy as we walk towards the tea-house by the Serpentine.

Allegory of Africa at the Albert Memorial (opposite)

Walk Four

Trafalgar Square – Whitehall – Horse Guards –
Banqueting House – Parliament Square – St Margaret's –
Westminster Abbey – St John, Smith Square –
Victoria Tower Gardens – Houses of Parliament –
Westminster Bridge – Albert Embankment –
Lambeth Palace – Tate Gallery – Westminster Cathedral –
Blewcoat School – St James's Park

Lord Nelson
on his Column

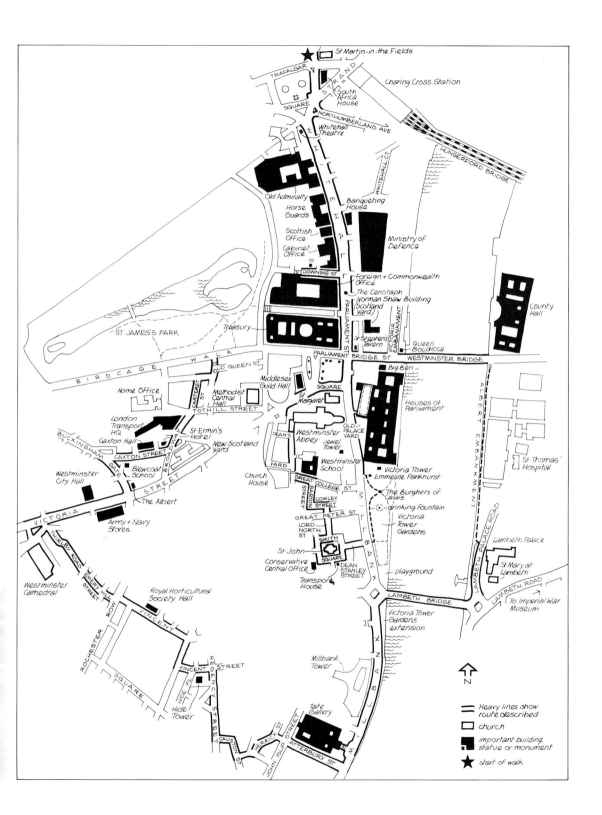

St Martin-in-the-Fields

Charing Cross Station

TRAFALGAR SQUARE

STRAND

South Africa House

Whitehall Theatre

NORTHUMBERLAND AVE

WHITEHALL CT

HUNGERFORD BRIDGE

Old Admiralty

Horse Guards

Banqueting House

Scottish Office

Ministry of Defence

Cabinet Office

10

DOWNING ST

Foreign + Commonwealth Office

The Cenotaph

Norman Shaw Building (Scotland Yard)

County Hall

ST JAMES'S PARK

Treasury

VICTORIA EMBANKMENT

St Stephen's Tavern

Queen Boudicca

BIRDCAGE WALK

PARLIAMENT ST

PARLIAMENT V

BRIDGE ST

WESTMINSTER BRIDGE

OLD QUEEN ST

Middlesex Guild Hall

SQUARE

Big Ben

Home Office

CAXTON ST

Methodist Central Hall

St Margaret

Houses of Parliament

ALBERT EMBANKMENT

London Transport HQ

TOTHILL STREET

St Ermin's Hotel

Caxton Hall

DEAN'S

Westminster Abbey

OLD PALACE YARD

BUCKINGHAM GATE

New Scotland Yard

YARD

Jewel Tower

St Thomas' Hospital

CAXTON STREET

Blewcoat School

BROADWAY

Westminster School

Victoria Tower

Emmeline Pankhurst

STREET

Westminster City Hall

Church House

GREAT COLLEGE ST

The Burghers of Calais

Lambeth Palace

VICTORIA

The Albert

BARTON STREET

COWLEY STREET

drinking fountain

Victoria Tower Gardens

St Mary at Lambeth

THIRLBY ROAD

Army + Navy Stores

GREAT PETER ST

LORD NORTH ST

SMITH SQUARE

LAMBETH ROAD

EMERY STREET

Westminster Cathedral

St John

playground

To Imperial War Museum

ROW

Royal Horticultural Society Hall

Conservative Central Office

DEAN STANLEY STREET

Transport House

LAMBETH BRIDGE

LAMBETH PALACE ROAD

ROCHESTER

VINCENT

VINCENT STREET

REGENCY STREET

Victoria Tower Gardens extension

SQUARE

HIDE PL

Millbank Tower

Hide Tower

MILLBANK

CAUSTON ST

HERRICK ST

JOHN ISLIP ST

Tate Gallery

ATTERBURY ST

N

—— Heavy lines show route described

☐ church

■ important building, statue or monument

★ start of walk

We start from the east side of the square, on the steps of St Martin's, and while we are passing the impassive frontage of South Africa House it could be diverting to muse upon what the square might have looked like had other plans been acceptable to Parliament. A certain Colonel Trench MP, who spent much of his life lobbying on behalf of various grandiose schemes for the enhancement, as he saw it, of London and its river, commissioned architects to design a pyramid as high as St Paul's Cathedral. One architect wished to place a Colosseum in the centre, another a cenotaph for Nelson in the Gothic style, and several envisaged temples. (The details may be found in Felix Barker and Ralph Hyde's *London As it Might Have Been*.)

As you wait to cross the road, which you must do twice, at Strand and Northumberland Avenue, observe the lamp-posts with cherubs cavorting about the uprights. Strand, meaning shore or bank, is so called because it was once much closer to the Thames than it has been since Bazalgette's Embankment was built in the mid nineteenth century. Northumberland Avenue is on the site of a Jacobean mansion of the same name belonging to the dukes and earls of the Percy family, the best remembered of whom is the one Shakespeare called Harry Hotspur. Although wide and tree-lined, and looking towards the Thames, it is a sombre thoroughfare. Not so Whitehall, by which we leave the square. This is even wider for most of its length but has curiously homely, even tatty, touches, to offset the grandeur of the government offices. But how did the gaunt and ghostly-looking Whitehall Theatre, for long the home of spicy revue, and after that of slapstick farce, get there, cheekily nudging the Admiralty and a solemn bank? And why haven't those decrepit buildings at the other end, where it briefly becomes Parliament Street, been removed or, at least, refurbished? These are the exceptions. Mostly Whitehall makes its importance felt, as a place with such a history should. Once it was covered by Whitehall Palace, the principle royal residence for about 160 years from the reign of Henry VIII until that of James II. Henry filched the grand house of Cardinal Wolsey when he fell from favour and it became his favourite residence. Charles I had plans for building something even grander which would have outdone most of his royal counterparts on the Continent and Inigo Jones was but one of the architects who submitted designs. Only Jones's Banqueting House, happily extant, was erected (1619–25) but Charles went on visualizing the palace of his dreams even when under sentence of death. Wren built a mansion by the Banqueting House for James II's Queen but it and much else was destroyed by fires in the 1690s.

The Foreign Office King Charles St (opposite)

Over the next two centuries government moved in on Whitehall which today boasts the Foreign and Commonwealth Office, the

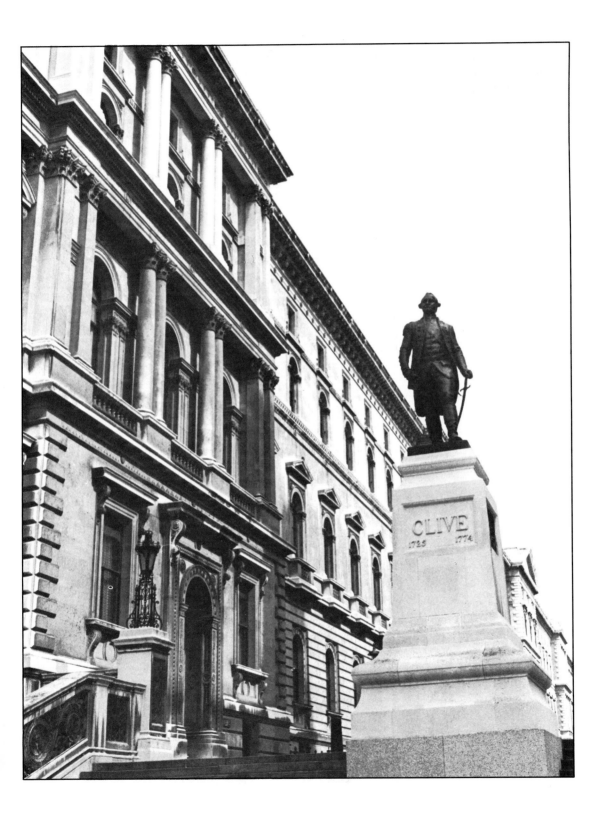

Admiralty, the Ministry of Defence, the Civil Service Department, the Cabinet Office and, of course, in a short street leading off, the Treasury and the Prime Minister's official residence. The Home Office has moved out to Queen Anne's Gate, and the police headquarters to Victoria Street.

At the start we walk down the east side, past souvenir shops and pubs, with Big Ben and the towers of Westminster in the distance. Opposite is the Admiralty with a screen by Robert Adam, and then the Horse Guards, one of the leading tourist attractions of London. Here the Changing of the Guards takes place at eleven each morning and the clicking of cameras is heard even above the roar of passing traffic. There are two regiments of guards involved, the Life, in red capes and white plumes, and the Royal, in blue tunics and red plumes. Both wear helmets with gold tassels and, when on duty, sit motionless but not, one supposes, totally impervious, otherwise what would be the point in their being there apart from attracting visitors? They are not allowed to converse but provided you do not touch them or their weapons they will allow themselves to be photographed. The Horse Guards is a most endearing mid-eighteenth-century building by William Kent always carrying the eye on easily to its domes and cupolas and pediments. It is even more handsome on the other side facing the spacious parade ground where the Queen reviews the Trooping of the Colour, an annual ceremony held each June, for which stands of seats are erected.

After the guard has been changed, and supposing you have crossed Whitehall to watch it, return to the east side to visit the Banqueting House. This simple and dignified two-storey building is imbued with Inigo Jones's dedication to the architectural principles of the Italian Renaissance. Jones made extensive and lengthy tours of Italy; we shall not meet much of his work on these walks and certainly nothing finer than this. The hall, on the higher floor, is a double cube, 110 feet long by 55 feet wide and high. There are eight columns either side with a balcony above the entrance and a throne at the far end, under a canopy, looking as though the stage has been set for an Elizabethan play. The ceiling was painted by Rubens and there are angled mirrors standing on the floor to aid inspection of it: unfortunately, it is difficult to see the paintings without looking at oneself. The subject is the apotheosis of the Stuart virtues of kingship and it says something for Oliver Cromwell's tolerance that they were not obliterated after Charles I had walked out from this very building to the scaffold. Eleven years later Charles's son was greeted here by members of both Houses of Parliament who offered him the crown.

For much of the eighteenth and nineteenth centuries the house was used as a chapel, although it was never consecrated. More recently it has reverted to an earlier use. Receptions are given to visiting delegations but not, I imagine, in as lavish a way as is described by Samuel Pepys and John Evelyn. At its southern end it is joined to the building of the Royal United Services Institution and from 1890 to 1963 was part of their war museum. It is open Tuesday–Saturday 10–5; Sunday 2–5. There is a charge for admission.

Cross Whitehall again, either at the Horse Guards or further down, because you will wish to look into Downing Street where the Prime Minister and the Chancellor of the Exchequer live, although not together. Next to the Horse Guards is Dover House which is the Scottish Office and, says Pevsner, 'the most elegant piece of architecture' in Whitehall. The buildings on this side, from here to Parliament Square, apart from what you can see of Dorset House and the Treasury, are intimidatingly bleak Victorian edifices calculated to fill the meek with a fear of officialdom. First comes the Cabinet Office (once the Treasury) which, for all that it has retained its Whitehall frontage has, apparently, been totally rebuilt behind it. The Foreign Office, beyond the entrance to Downing Street, has remained in its purpose-built premises, and annexed those of the Home Office, to make room for the Commonwealth Office with which it was amalgamated some years ago. Twice I have been inside it. Once I ascended to a gloomy Gothic attic, which I reached by treading many corridors of power, to visit the librarian in a room which might have been a monk's cell. Another time I was at a reception in the Foreign Secretary's own office, a spacious and gracious chamber overlooking St James's Park. And it is not so many years since I was permitted to drive into Downing Street, turn left under an archway into the great inner courtyard of the FO, and deliver books. Nowadays, when the police have been forced into taking greater care of senior ministers, you will be fortunate if you are allowed as far as the famous door of No. 10 without special authority, and there is a barrier to stop vehicles.

The Prime Minister's residence looks comparatively modest from outside but spreads widely behind other buildings in the street. It has an enclosed, walled garden familiar from all those formal photographs of cabinet groups. Some PMs are more lavish in their entertaining than others. Harold Wilson liked to invite people from all walks of life to his receptions and during his time many more citizens saw something of the interior of No. 10 than has been customary since. During his second term of office Mary Wilson refused to live there and they settled in Lord North Street to which we shall come later; otherwise all prime ministers from the first, Robert Walpole, have resided here. Most of us have to be content with the glimpses of life in this famous house as revealed in many volumes of memoirs, or from the detailed description by Professor Pevsner who, deservedly, got in everywhere.

We pass on to Parliament Square noting, almost opposite, the grey hulk of the Ministry of Defence which started life as the Air Ministry. It need not delay us although you may wish to cross the road yet again to admire the statues of Monty (Field Marshal Lord Montgomery of Alamein) and of Sir Walter Raleigh – with cloak. In wide Whitehall itself there are several, mostly equestrian, statues to less memorable men but also to Field Marshal Haig, under whose command millions died in Flanders. He received an earldom and a large cheque; the slaughtered got Sir Edwin Lutyens's Cenotaph, a simple-looking white monument at which royalty and political leaders lay wreaths once a year. In fact the Cenotaph stands in Parliament Street, not in Whitehall – it really would be simpler if the road had one name throughout. However, off Parliament Street, as we must call it, is Scotland Yard, the police headquarters for most of a century, and its adjoining New Scotland Yard. This leads to a further confusion of nomenclature because the cops, in fact, have gone off to Victoria Street, as already mentioned, to a new HQ which they also call New Scotland Yard. The earlier buildings are now named, after their architect, Norman Shaw Building North and South but the narrow street leading to them is still Scotland Yard, and it will be a long time before it is dissociated in the public mind from the home of the law.

Parliament Square, with Big Ben and the Houses of Parliament on your left as you enter, and opposite, Westminster Abbey, apparently clutching the diminutive-looking church of St Margaret unto itself, presents a pleasing composition across a spread of green. Not all grass, of course, because provision has to be made for traffic, and also for statuary. There is Palmerston upstanding, Churchill stooping, Smuts (the Boer leader who became pro-British) leaning forward, and Disraeli (here called Beaconsfield) and Derby, looking dandyish. A fourth Victorian premier, Robert Peel, who was responsible for introducing both income tax and the police (hence Bobbies), is also here, as is a fifth, George Canning, got up as a Roman. He is outside the Middlesex Guildhall, along with Abraham Lincoln, whose statue is a copy of one in Chicago. But why is Lincoln here at all? Perhaps to remind us that the United States, like South Africa, was once a colony, just as the Guildhall recalls the long status of Middlesex as a county.

It is possible to reach the centre of the square – just – thanks to zebra crossings and strategically placed traffic lights, and also to return from it on the south side to visit St Margaret's where fashionable weddings take place. John Milton was married here, so was Samuel Pepys and, in this century, Winston Churchill. William Caxton (more of him later) was buried here, and Sir Walter Raleigh,

Protecting the Premier
Downing Street
(opposite)

and a great many others whose tombs lie 'thick as autumnal leaves/in Vallombrosa', or, as Milton might have added in a different context, 'statues in Westminster Abbey'. Some of them are singular indeed. One is like a Punch and Judy show with figures confronting each other in an inset; another is of Francis Egioke, Jacobean gentleman, cut off at the knees (as was the fashion) in a kind of theatre box; a third has a plaintive plea beneath it – 'I pray you remember Henry Austen Layard, P.C., G.C.B., Discoverer of Nineveh.'

Leave St Margaret's, which is sited to make it a foil for its larger neighbour, by the west (main) door to gain a view, through trees, of Methodist Central Hall (an indoor meeting-place for those who rally in Trafalgar Square, as well as for the faithful) over in Storey's Gate. Then turn to observe the tower of St Margaret's which stands apart like an Italian campanile, and note the pretty blue facings on the sun clock. The church dates back at least to the early twelfth century and has been restored, altered and repaired as much as any building as old as that. It is the parish church of Parliament.

Enter the Abbey by the main door, under the twin towers which by failing to soar off into the outer atmosphere belittle an otherwise fine building. Your disappointment can be quickly overcome by seeing the great sweep of nave and crossing, and the vaulting. Is it greater or finer than a score of other Gothic cathedrals you have experienced? Not, perhaps, at the moment but there is wondrous matter to come and, anyhow, is it possible to tire of even the 'ordinary' in this genre? Architectural details I will not attempt. The Abbey is one of the most recorded buildings in Britain, and has been for centuries.

As in St Margaret's, there are signs in the Abbey commanding No Lecturing, No Photography. This may seem illiberal at those times of year when visitors are comparatively few in number, but it is pleasant to be relieved of the so-often dogmatically assertive and necessarily stentorian voice of the guide, and of the flashing of bulbs.

Who first put a church here, we do not know. It could have been a colony of monks on the Island of Thorns amidst the marshes. They may have built an abbey. What we do know is that Edward the Confessor, king of England from 1042 until the epoch-making year of 1066, rebuilt one in time for the arrival of William the Conqueror. Edward was canonized; William was not, but there can be no doubt about who had the greater influence.

Roman remains have been found on the site of the Abbey which has nine hundred years of recorded history. It bears the marks of having been lived in, or worshipped in, by every royal dynasty from the Normans onwards. Here our monarchs are crowned and our great buried. Here you may see the fine nave built by Henry Yevele, our first named architect. He lived in the fourteenth century and escaped the Black Death. His nave replaced the Norman one and he, with Henry Harland, reconstructed Westminster Hall to which we come later. You can also see the breathtaking fan vaulting of the Henry VII chapel, an extension of the Abbey which is truly a building in itself.

There are guided Super Tours of the Abbey several times each day for £2.50 and they are what you should take unless you are the sort who likes to nose things out independently, in which case come with me, for a start, and note, after your first overall and lengthy acceptance of the interior as a whole (so far as you can see it), some detail.

On the left as you enter are flagstones commemorating Clement Attlee, David Lloyd George, Beatrice and Sidney Webb, Ramsay Macdonald and Ernest Bevin, but where is Asquith? To the right of them, as is proper though political, is Winston Churchill.

The clutter of memorials leaves what you have seen in St Margaret's as a mere sketch for the bureaucracy of death. No one seems to have foreseen what the population explosion would mean. (Significantly, there is no monument to Malthus.) Had they done so, would they have been content with smaller monuments? Perhaps not.

To visit the rear of the Abbey you must pay £1.20. This admits you to the glories of the Henry VII chapel and also into side chapels where there is evidence of overcrowding. In the Elizabeth Chapel there is one huge tomb with Good Queen Bess on top of her sister Mary, and little room to ease around it; on the opposite side, after leaving Henry VII, you find the other Mary crammed with all her family into an exquisitely designed chamber, the proportions and decorations of which are ruined by the monstrously baroque sarcophagus to the Queen of Scots. The fact that it is here says something about religious tolerance at one level but, had circumstances been different, would the same have been done for Gloriana, one wonders? Ecumenicalism had not then, I think, been much encouraged.

You should not let such considerations mar your appreciation of Henry's chapel which is hung with the standards of the Sovereign and of the Knights of the Order of the Bath, a hangover from more heraldic days, but still meaningful to those belonging or aspiring to it. The knights' armoured headpieces, with tassels hanging from them, are above the stalls. Certainly the standards add to the splendour of the scene. Oliver Cromwell is buried just in front of an inner chapel dedicated to the pilots of the Battle of Britain who are also remembered in a stained-glass window. (And note the tomb of Almeric de Courcy, Lord Kinsale, with two cherubs holding up his couch.)

To reach the tomb of Edward the Confessor a bridge has been constructed, with one-way traffic, designed to channel visitors in orderly file. At the entrance to the chamber is Henry V lying on his back and giving a passable imitation of Laurence Olivier; then there is Edward's enormous mausoleum in three great chunks of stone, the topmost of which is like a model for a *commedia dell'arte* stage setting. The Coronation Chair, made in 1300, is here behind bars (although in the past it has been bedecked with graffiti) with the Stone of Scone, the symbol of Scottish monarchy, intact beneath it after its absence in the 1950s when it was stolen by patriots. Above the chair is a stone wall of the fifteenth century with scenes from the life of Edward on its cornice.

Go from here to the already-mentioned Mary Chapel where, incongruously, there is also a slab to the memory of Cecil Rhodes, the Victorian adventurer whose name has only recently disappeared from the maps of Africa. Then down to Poets' Corner which is by no means solely for those who versified. George as well as T. S. Eliot is here, as are Handel and Congreve.

In the cloisters beyond the brass-rubbing industry flourishes, as in so many religious centres, and there are more sarcophagi. Before leaving via the exit to Dean's Yard go to the eastern side of the cloisters and into the Chapter House. This was being constructed in the thirteenth century at the same time as the abbey but the iron roof belongs to the nineteenth. This octagonal chamber of great beauty and simplicity was, for two centuries, used by the Commons as their Parliament House. There is a small extra charge for visiting it, as there is for the Abbey Treasures, situated next door. The Chapter House is well worth it; the Treasures, in my view, vulgarize a great ecclesiastical building.

When you come out follow the cloisters round until you are near to the west end of the Abbey and then step out into Dean's Yard, a quiet enclave with a grassy centre and soft surrounding buildings. At the south end is Church House, decorated with various crests and showing a foundation stone laid by Queen Mary in 1937. On the east side and spreading beyond the frontage is Westminster School, which began as an attachment to a Benedictine monastery. In 1461 it moved here where it has remained ever since although as much altered and rebuilt as its neighbours. In the worst fire raid of the Second World War on Westminster it suffered especially and the renovated premises were not officially reopened until 1950.

Leave Dean's Yard by a passage under the buildings next to Church House and turn left into Great College Street, then right into Barton Street where, at No. 14, there is a plaque to T. E. Lawrence. Barton becomes Cowley Street at a right angle in an area which maintains the cloistered atmosphere of the Yard. There is another right angle in Cowley Street from which you have your first view of St John, Smith Square, an almost square baroque church with two high porticoed entrances and four ornately decorated towers topped with what appear to be stone thistles. It has excited much derisive comment in its time (Dickens likened it to a petrified monster with its legs in the air, others called it Queen Anne's footstool because that lady when quarrelling with an architect is alleged to have kicked her stool on to its back and said, 'build me a church like that then'). By the end of the last war it was a charred ruin and remained such until the mid 1960s when it was lovingly restored but not reconsecrated. Instead it was dedicated to music. Lunchtime concerts to which the public is admitted free of charge are broadcast from here by the BBC.

To reach St John's we cross Great Peter Street into Lord North Street, as fine a Georgian street as you will find anywhere around here. Surprisingly, considering the distinguished men and women who have lived in it, there are no plaques. The church dominates Smith Square where, on one corner, is Transport House, for long the

Division Bell territory
Smith Square

headquarters of the Labour Party but now occupied solely by the powerful union which owns it. The Conservative and Unionist Party Central Office is also in the square which we leave by Dean Stanley Street, noting another pleasing early-eighteenth-century terrace on the north side.

Cross busy Millbank to Victoria Tower Gardens, a lunchtime haven for office workers beside the Thames. It has a playground at the Lambeth Bridge end and also a Gothic drinking fountain (for humans not horses) placed there to commemorate the emancipation of slaves in 1834. Its roof is unsuitably painted in garish colours. Nearer the Palace of Westminster is a copy of Rodin's powerful group, *The Burghers of Calais*, celebrating a famous incident in Anglo-French relations when mercy triumphed. The channel port had been starved into surrender by Edward III who demanded the lives of its six leading citizens: his queen interceded successfully for them. At the Abingdon Street exit there is a lovely statue of the pioneer suffragette, Emmeline Pankhurst. It was erected by her daughter, Dame Christabel. Mrs Pankhurst and the Burghers lie in the shadow of Victoria Tower which now holds those parliamentary records formerly in the Jewel Tower across the main road (Pevsner calls it a 'trumpet blast'). Its height (334 feet) only emphasizes the squatness of the Abbey's west-front towers which can only just be seen from here.

For seventy years the Jewel Tower, built by Henry Yevele, was used by the Board of Trade as a Weights and Measures Office. Since its restoration in 1956 it has been opened to the public. To visit it involves two crossings of a fast road so you may prefer to stay beside Old Palace Yard before going into the Houses of Parliament.

The Palace of Westminster is on the site of what was the sovereign's home until Whitehall Palace was built. The only remaining part of the early royal residence is Westminster Hall with its magnificent hammer-beam roof. When royalty moved out the various buildings which had comprised the palace were used as administrative offices and law courts. Within the area were shops, inns, houses. Gradually, over the centuries, it became the meeting-place of both the Lords and then the Commoners as they gained greater influence over government. In the eighteenth and early nineteenth centuries new buildings arose but it was not until after the fire of 1834 that the Houses of Parliament, as we know them, came into being as purpose-built premises. The principal architects were Charles Barry and Augustus Pugin, and a fine Gothic pile they made of it, with the four-pinnacled Victoria Tower at one end, and the clock tower of Big Ben at the other. Between them, encompassing Westminster Hall and various courts, is the long, majestic, symmetrical agglomeraton of debating chambers, libraries, lobbies, committee and robing rooms, offices, restaurants, bars and galleries which face the river with two more lower towers at each end. The conception is lofty, the detail intricate and meticulously executed. From without, especially from Westminster Bridge or the south bank, it is unthinkable that anything should be allowed to replace this familiar and well-loved palace, the symbol of the nation's belief in democracy. Inside it can give you the horrors with its narrow rooms and high ceilings, its spiral staircases and dark passages, and its vast ill-lit central lobby resembling the departure forecourt of a railway terminal in wartime. The chamber of the House of Commons especially strikes one as being absurdly small and, of course, it is, not having enough seats for all of its 650 members. It was burned out by enemy bombs in 1941, when the roof was also destroyed, but the opportunity this offered, of rebuilding it with sufficient accommodation for all members, was missed: it was restored, with pious love, to its former glory. The Lords is also inadequately provided with seats for its one thousand and more members but this is of lesser importance because many of them do not attend often, or even ever. Yet the fees payable to their lordships for looking in daily when sessions are in progress attract more than of yore and, in any case, many of them are nowadays ennobled for the purpose of governing alongside whichever party is in power.

There are guided tours on certain days when Parliament is not sitting, and on some mornings when it is. The public is admitted to the House of Commons, the House of Lords, the Queen's Robing Room, the Prince's Chamber, the Peers' Lobby, the Royal Gallery, the Crypt Chapel, Westminster Hall and other corridors and lobbies. Saturday is a safe choice because sessions are only very rarely held on that day; also Bank Holiday Mondays and the Tuesdays following them. However, if you know a member or a worker in the house a visit can usually be arranged, and if you wish to attend a debate you can apply at the Admission Order Office in the Central Lobby for a place in the Strangers' Gallery. You may have a long wait.

Coming from Victoria Tower Gardens you pass the Lords and the equestrian statue of Richard I with his sword raised high above him, and another to Cromwell, who has a lion couchant below the plinth on which he stands. As with the tomb to Mary Queen of Scots, but perhaps more so, foreigners may wonder that the Lord Protector, who ordered the execution of King Charles I, should be honoured in so conspicuous a place, but it must be understood that Cromwell was a parliamentarian first and foremost, not a wild revolutionary, certainly not a terrorist in the contemporary sense, and it was only following

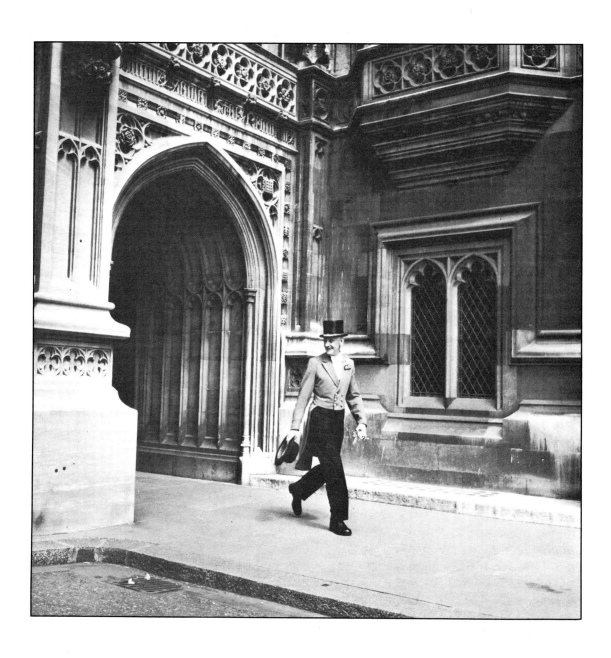

Hats
House of Lords

his natural death that the monarchy was restored. He was not deposed, and Parliament looks after its own, which is why it is said to be one of the best clubs in London. Members of all parties mingle socially however aggressively they may behave to each other on the floor of the House. And they guard their privileges keenly. Some of the ceremonies seen on television when the State Opening of Parliament by the Queen is shown strike me as more than faintly ludicrous. The British love of fancy dress comes abundantly into play as the newly ennobled arrive in their ermine and glad rags to take their places in the Lords, but the most famous ritual is that in which a person called Black Rod, dressed to look like an aged actor-manager playing Hamlet, struts from the Lords to the Commons and has the door slammed in his face. This symbolizes (I think) that the Commons are the elected representatives of the people and not at the beck and call of the Lords, or even the Crown. The rituals and business have been evolved over hundreds of years – some of it is still written out in Norman French, which only some three living scholars can understand – and it has all worked modestly well for us British although we have not exported it with very favourable results. There are those who think that some modernization both of premises and procedure would do the home-bred product no harm.

We seek admittance at St Stephen's entrance and, in the porch, we are screened for explosives and other lethal offerings. On our left is Westminster Hall, built for William II (Rufus) between 1097 and 1099, and rebuilt for Richard II some three hundred years later. It is 240 feet long and, in its central part, rises to 92 feet. It has withstood not only the ravages of man, but of the deathwatch beetle and of a bomb attack as short a time ago as 1974. The latter did much damage but also provided archaeologists with evidence of human occupation (possibly Iron Age) on what was known in early Christian times as Thorney Island. The underground car-park built at approximately the same time in the 1970s also provided evidence of earlier buildings.

But you may not go into the hall without an escort. If you are meeting an MP or worker in the House you go to the Central Lobby where there are statues to Churchill, Lloyd George, and Attlee. Who, I wonder, will get the presently vacant fourth position? It may be going to the Member you have come to meet.

After our visit we leave the Palace to its legislation and points of order, stay briefly in Parliament Square, then turn right into Bridge Street with Big Ben above us. The first clock tower near the site was also by Yevele and lasted over three hundred years until Wren pulled it down, sending its bell, known as 'Great Tom' to St Paul's where, in recast form, it still is. If for any reason the chimes of Big Ben (possibly named after a Victorian prize fighter) are not available to the BBC, it uses Great Tom's instead. The lower rooms of the clock tower were traditionally used for the detention of errant members but the last person confined there was the atheist Bradlaugh, who refused to testify on the Bible in 1880. Recently I visited the political adviser to the Leader of the Opposition, who has been given a cell there, disguised as an office.

In Bridge Street is St Stephen's Tavern where the division bells ring in case imbibing Members are inside when a vote is called. At the junction of Bridge Street with Victoria Embankment is an enormous statue of Queen Boadicea (Boudicca) on her chariot. She, as Queen of the Iceni, sacked Roman London. They say that Margaret Thatcher stands in front of her supplicating guidance.

We go on to Westminster Bridge, the view seaward from which is spoiled by Hungerford Bridge, which takes trains into Charing Cross. Most of the bridges across the Thames are pleasing in one style or another, so it is a pity that the bombs which closed several tracks of this one in 1944 did not complete the job. Even so, pause and think of Wordsworth ('Earth hath not anything to show more fair') and shed a tear. And another as you look at the colossal edifice on the other bank, the palatial building with the central, curving colonnade. This is County Hall, a monument to superfluous bureaucracy, the home of the now-doomed Greater London Council. County Hall, when it has been disbanded, will become a conference centre, or art gallery, or house some of London's destitute.

At the southern end of the bridge there are steps down to the Albert Embankment from which there is an undisturbed view of the Houses of Parliament. Walk along towards Lambeth Bridge with St Thomas's Hospital on your left for most of the way. It is not much to look at from the back (or from the front for that matter) apart from an Italianate tower with an iron balcony high upon it, so concentrate, instead, on the riparian view of what is visible, which is partly explained on a plaque. Only partly, because the diagram is not panoramic so you must guess where on the horizon is, say, New Covent Garden. Where the embankment path rejoins the road is Lambeth Palace, home of the Archbishop of Canterbury, which is one of those British things you just have to accept. It isn't even on the Dover Road. It is a red-brick, basically Tudor structure of great charm and it includes a chapel and a fortress-style gateway through which, alas, one may not pass, except on official or personal business. Beside the Palace is the church of St Mary-at-Lambeth, with a fourteenth-century tower, and that you may be lucky enough to visit. The church has escaped demolition thanks to the Tradescant Trust which is restoring it as a Museum of Garden History in memory of the two John Tradescants who are buried here. They were gardeners to Charles I and in the small churchyard there grow varieties of plants

Queen Boadicea
advancing on Parliament
Victoria Embankment
(opposite)

which they introduced into this country. Visiting hours vary Lambeth Palace
depending on the exigencies of the restoration.

That is Lambeth, so far as we are concerned in this walk, although the military-minded will wish to know about the Imperial War

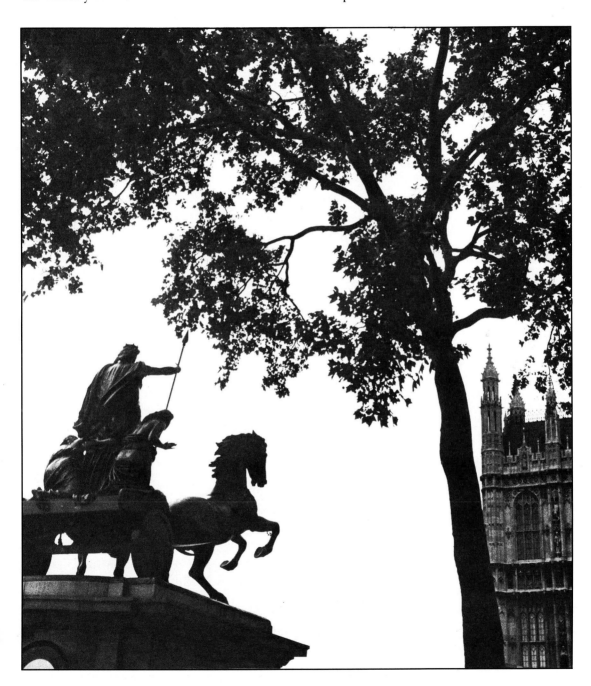

Museum about ten minutes' away in an easterly direction. It is open all weekdays and Sundays at the usual times, and is devoted to every aspect of war in the twentieth century.

Cross Lambeth Bridge back to the north bank and turn left into a short extension of Victoria Tower Gardens leading to Millbank, on the land side of which is an impressive item of modern engineering, Millbank Tower. It is of steel, glass and concrete, and part of it is supported on pillars which disclose an area of greenery and a car-park. The shape is interesting but the detail monotonous and, inevitably, in this capital city where land is at a premium, it is much too tall for its surroundings.

The Tate Gallery (which is why we are here) is in stark contrast and you might mistake it for an enlargement of one of the treasuries at Delphi. The frontage, up a dozen steps or so, is rather too grand for the height of the dwarfish building but inside is a fine collection. After the baggage search you pass into a circular inner vestibule where there are alcoves with round tables. Here you can sit and plan your visit to this gallery, on the site of a Victorian prison. It was given to the nation by a sugar millionaire, Sir Henry Tate, and to his original collection of Victorian paintings and sculptures so much has been added that it is impossible to display all that has been entrusted to it. The Tate is especially important as the despository of nearly twenty thousand works – paintings, sketches and drawings – by J. M. W. Turner, a selection of which is always on view. It is rich also in British painting of this and earlier centuries. William Blake is well represented, as are Samuel Palmer, Reynolds, Constable, Gainsborough, Stubbs, the pre-Raphaelites, Stanley Spencer and many others. However, it would be inaccurate to identify the Tate solely with British art or with contemporary work, although it is much associated with both. Periodically the gallery receives publicity from that section of the press which likes to pander to the latent philistinism of its readership. Thus, when the Tate acquires some construction which doesn't instantly accord with the average person's conception of a work of art, it is reviled for alleged misuse of public funds. I cannot pretend to be enthusiastic about the brick wall which was the object of journalistic outcries a few years ago, or about many of the modern paintings and sculptures on display, but it is necessary for artists to experiment, and warnings about the emperor's new clothes should be heard only if adverse contemporary opinions of what are now accepted masterpieces are also allowed. What is invariably overlooked in press tirades against the Tate's recent acquisitions is the wonderful variety and intrinsic value of the greater part of the collection.

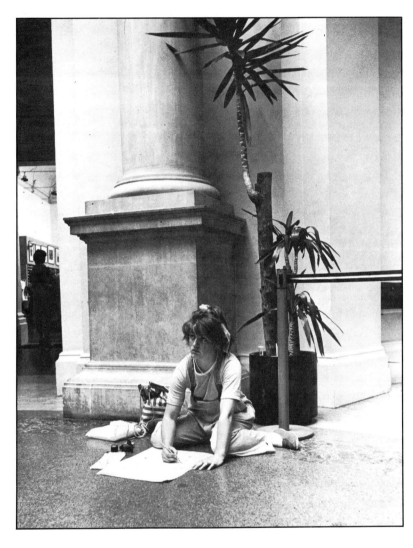

Copying a Master
Tate Gallery

The impressionists and post-impressionists (and who can confidently say into which category many of those so described should go?) form only a part of the foreign collection which is well endowed with examples of fauvism, cubism, surrealism, dada, pop and many manifestations of abstract art. There is, besides, much sculpture with the accent, once again, on British work.

During school term-time, as in other galleries, there are usually groups of kids making copies or notes, or listening to lecturers. The ones who listen have every chance of understanding art. I heard a young instructor with a splendid canvas-side approach talking about one of the large boldly coloured Matisses one day, and paused to pick up what I could. It reminded me of my first approach to painting when the wartime woman art teacher sent to my boys' school at Tunbridge Wells, in 1943, took a class of us to an exhibition of the work of Feliks Topolski. 'Do you like him, Miss?' I earnestly enquired. 'I don't know that I should like to *live* with him,' she replied. (Well, we'd gossiped about her and the French teacher, but that was a bit bald.) I don't know that I would like to live with all that number of the contemporary canvases at the Tate but I am grateful that they are there.

There is a well-stocked book, print and slide department and the restaurant, with decorations by Rex Whistler, is highly praised. Apart from the permanent collection there are regular exhibitions of new or retrospective work and in the garden is statuary by Henry Moore and Barbara Hepworth, on one side, and a full-size figure of Sir John Millais, looking like a Victorian banker, on the other. Open all weekdays 10–6, Sundays 2–6.

The next ten minutes of this walk will be very dull so concentrate your mind on some of the lovely paintings you have seen, perhaps asking yourself if Turner's views of Venice aren't superior to Canaletto's, as you walk up Atterbury Street, past an entrance to the gallery for the disabled, and into the Millbank council estate where what were once thought of as high-rise blocks are named after English painters and other famous men. Cross John Islip Street into Herrick Street, wend your way round leftwards into Causton Street (there was an Elizabethan composer of that name), where you turn right, and into Regency Street where you turn right again. Pass Hide Tower (modern, on stilts) in Hide Place, on your left, then turn left into Vincent Street leading into Vincent Square. Here you get the first view of the Byzantine tower of the Roman Catholic Westminster Cathedral, to reach which is the purpose of this detour.

Vincent Square belongs to Westminster School. It is their playing-field. On what is roughly the north side of it we go past the Royal Horticultural Hall and across Rochester Row into Emery Hill Street and Thirlby Road (an area of prosperous high-class tenements which are called apartments), where we turn left just before encountering Glassomania. The road shoots under a jazzy contemporary structure which ends to make room for a piazza from Victoria Street leading to the cathedral and making it, after all these decades, the end of a vista. It is the one real improvement in this quite disastrously redeveloped region of London which was never beautiful, but is now quite notoriously ugly. However, before enduring more of it, turn into the piazza where there are benches from which you can look up at the 284-foot-high campanile surmounted by a cupola with a Moorish balcony midway up. The red brick interlaced with lines of white stone is a gorgeous architectural feast, all the better for being only partly uniform and for having a variety of endlessly engaging detail.

Of the interior, Service comments, 'a huge and calm space . . . one of the noblest of English churches'. In *The Buildings of England* we read, 'The interior is without a doubt one of the most moving of any churches in London.' David Piper refers to 'a grandeur that I find perennially and undiminishedly astonishing'; Jones and Woodward call it 'impressive'. So it has to be one of my blind spots. To me it is dark and drab with many side chapels guarded by bleak railings, and everywhere there is marble in such a variety of different grains that you might think yourself in some gigantic sample shop. In front of the altar is a pavilion that would look at home in the grounds of a stately mansion and there is a truly frightful pulpit. It is made of marble and mosaic and resembles a chunk of icing sugar blended with lurid confections which have gone heavily to its candy-stick legs. But I do like a side chapel to the right of the altar where the bright gold and yellow mosaic rises up the wall and over the ceiling ending in a half dome. It reminds me of Ravenna and Monreale.

The Stations of the Cross in the nave are by Eric Gill and are highly regarded but this cathedral is so gloomy that they are difficult to see. I am glad to reach the piazza again and enjoy the ravishing exterior.

And so to Victoria Street with its demented skyscrapers, among them to the right Westminster City Hall and the new Army and Navy Stores. Standing dignified, far below them all, on the corner of Buckingham Gate, is a Victorian pub, the Albert (who else?). It is strange how often pubs escape the ravages of redevelopment. Perhaps the planners have some lingering sense of the necessity of allowing the ordinary citizen to cling to the familiar. The Albert has newly rendered dark brickwork and smartly painted fascia boards, advertising Barley Wine, Plymouth Gin, etc. Above the fourth, top, floor, is an elaborate cornice. Long live Albert.

Just off Buckingham Gate, to the right, in an irregularly shaped courtyard, stands another sight for by now very sore eyes, the early eighteenth-century Blewcoat School – one storey and cellar – belonging to the National Trust who open it as a gift shop for several weeks before Christmas. It may be visited at other times on application to the secretary.

Turn right, into Caxton Street in which is Caxton Hall, belonging to Westminster City Council, a well-known registry office for weddings. (In fashionable terms it is a secular St Margaret's for top people.) Caxton crops up hereabout because it was in Westminster that William Caxton set up the first printing press in England in 1476,

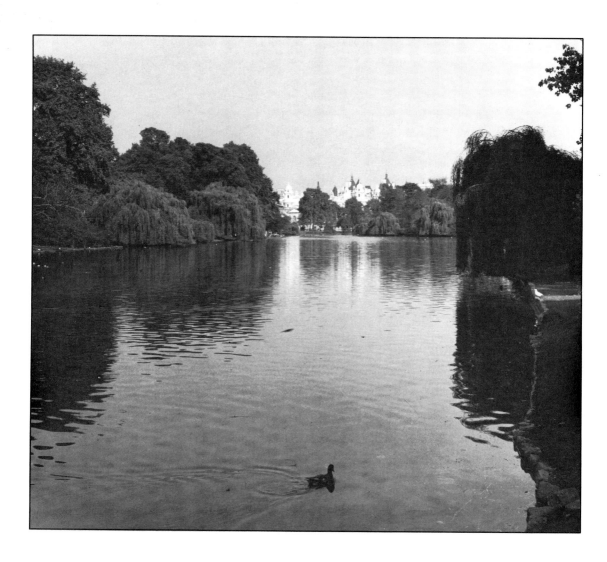

The towers of Whitehall from St James's Park

somewhere in the Abbey precincts at the sign of the Red Pale, where he worked for about fifteen years, not only as printer, but as author, translator, bookseller and publisher. He was the first complete bookman.

As you pass along Caxton Street and into The Broadway note the St Ermin's Hotel with strange heraldic beasts as guardians on its gateposts. In the Broadway is St James's Park Tube Station, and the headquarters of London Transport, a vast dignified building in granite by Charles Holden, a twentieth-century architect who understood the need to give variety to a large building. In this instance the variety includes sculptures by Gill, Moore, etc. Holden, with the enthusiastic support of Frank Pick, London Transport's chief executive between the wars, designed not only 55, The Broadway, but many underground stations, some of which, in the suburbs especially, are the only signs of architectural distinction over hundreds of acres. We shall meet his work again in Walk Six when we reach London University.

From Broadway into Tothill Street, and a view of the Abbey. Then left into Carteret Street (plaques to F. E. Smith, politician, and Lord Fisher, sailor) and down Cockpit Steps into Old Queen Street which gives access to Birdcage Walk and St James's Park. Here you may rest by the lake shaped like a bone after a dog has gnawed at it, and enjoy the vista of Whitehall Court above the government offices. On the lake are two small islands which are bird sanctuaries, and the park itself is liberally endowed with trees, shrubs and flowers. It is a favourite lunchtime retreat for office workers, and much used also by cabinet ministers (trailed by press photographers) for 'relaxing' walks before facing the Commons.

Walk Five

Market Hall
Covent Garden
(opposite)

Trafalgar Square – St Martin-in-the-Fields –
St Martin's Lane – Covent Garden – Bow Street –
Drury Lane – Aldwych – Waterloo Bridge – South Bank –
Strand – Charing Cross – Embankment Gardens

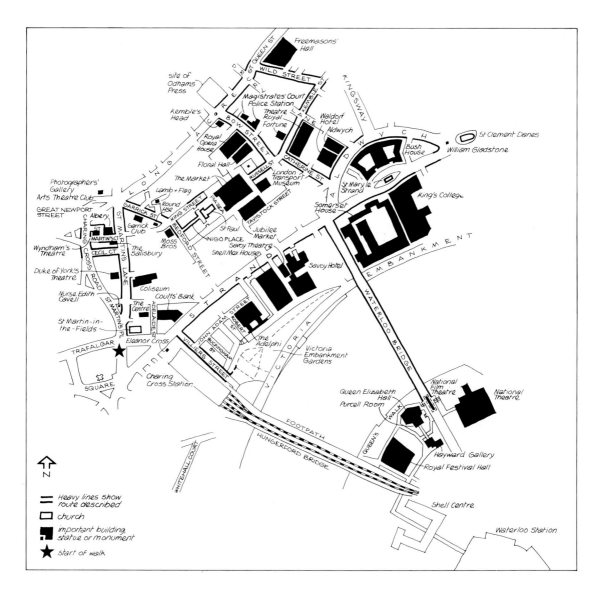

Again we start on the steps of St Martin-in-the-Fields, but this time we go inside behind the six noble columns supporting the portico. A spacious church, built by James Gibbs in the 1720s, on a site hallowed since the early thirteenth century, and perhaps before, it is arguably the best known in London. This is because of its long association with broadcasting, its musical eminence through the Academy of St Martin-in-the-Fields and the ministry of Dick Sheppard (1914–27). Enter through a lobby where there is a bookstall into a wide nave with a gallery on pillars on three sides. The ceiling is in cream and brown panels with gold and white mouldings and many endearing cherubs. The window above the altar is simple with small leaded panes, twenty-eight of which are picked out in blue to form a cross. To the left is a royal box, in the foreground, to the right an oak pulpit (possibly by Grinling Gibbons) standing on a single broad pillar balanced by a delicately carved, curving staircase.

Sheppard became Vicar after serving for three months on the Western Front. He identified himself with the people of his parish, and with those passing through it, so wholeheartedly that his church became crowded for services, and his crypt packed with the poor, the sick, the destitute. St Martin's became known as 'The Church Which Cares', a reputation still proudly maintained. Sheppard was something of an actor and also a humourist: there was laughter in his church, as well as worship and music.

The crypt and its surrounding rooms were once a burial ground. Nell Gwynn, mistress of Charles II, was entombed here at her own request, as were the artist Nicholas Hilliard and the craftsman Thomas Chippendale. Here the caring ministry begun by Sheppard was continued by Austen Williams and by his successors whose work has overflowed into Adelaide Street and St Martin's Place. A Chinese congregation meets in the crypt, and so do musical groups. It is also soup kitchen, dormitory, rest room, rehearsal room and, above all, sanctuary. In St Martin's Place a social service unit has a full-time staff of eight plus nearly fifty part-timers. It is open from 10 a.m. to 9 p.m. on weekdays, and a skeleton staff is on duty at weekends to deal with the endless problems of the needy – alcoholics, the mentally distressed, drop-outs, drug addicts. In Adelaide Street, in what was a secondary school, is The Centre, a family membership club for young people over 16 but under 25. There is also a nursery school.

The church, like the crypt, is a sanctuary, and not only for worshippers. Look in at almost any time and you will see poor ragged, downtrodden creatures resting or asleep in the pews. Frequently it is also a centre of music. Its acoustics are perfect. The choir and

Academy broadcast regularly (under Sheppard it was the first church from which a service went on the air) and there are lunchtime concerts twice each week. The Academy was formed in 1959, and has recorded widely under its conductor Neville Marriner.

When you leave St Martin's strike north with, on your left, the statue to Nurse Edith Cavell who, in 1914, was in charge of a Red Cross hospital in Brussels when the Germans occupied Belgium. She assisted allied soldiers to escape and proudly confessed to doing so when tried by the Germans, who then shot her. On her statue are her last words, 'Patriotism is not enough'.

Enter St Martin's Lane where the Coliseum, the home of the English National Opera Company, dominates the lower part of the street. It was built in 1903 by Frank Matcham who specialized in theatrical baroquery and red plush interiors. It began life as a music-hall. The globe which surmounts its tower enhances the roofscape. Almost opposite is the smaller, more sedate Duke of York's Theatre where the first London performance of *Peter Pan* was given in December 1904. It has a pretty balcony on to the street and its typically Victorian interior has been refurbished because modern audiences would not tolerate the discomfort formerly endured by generations of pit-and-gallery-ites. There is a strong theatrical flavour to this walk which takes in at least sixteen play and opera houses, although not each of them is mentioned.

Turn left into Cecil Court, a paved way through to Charing Cross Road. It has small shops on both sides and most of them sell books: new, secondhand and antiquarian. During the eight or nine decades of its existence many engaging eccentrics have traded here, and some still do, but there is a tendency nowadays, for economic reasons, to take the job of bookselling more earnestly. Rents are higher than of yore, and so are personal aspirations to comfort and leisure. So the paintpots have been out and some of the little shops are spruce and gleaming. Others, still dingy inside and out, are, nevertheless, specialists in their fields. It is an agreeable stretch of traffic-free territory in which to linger before turning right, briefly, into Charing Cross Road, the home of bigger, brighter booksellers, most of whom trade in newly published volumes at the top of the street, which is not on the official route. That it is not, I regret, because Charing Cross Road and its bookshops, new and secondhand, was the haunt of my childhood, the place to which I made hotfoot, eager especially for the splendid disarray of Foyle's where amongst a hundred heaps of old volumes or on many an undusted shelf, I would have to make an agonized choice between several titles. Now Foyle's has been cleaned up and has escalators, and the more decrepit of its two buildings has

Garrick Theatre
Charing Cross Road
(see Walk Six)

been sold to a competitor who has fitted it with carpets and new shelving. Lower down the street the dowdy, curving blocks, housing more bookshops, with the tenements and courts of Peabody Buildings behind them, look ripe for development. Architecturally their passing could not be regretted but the bookish face of Charing Cross Road would be changed forever. However there is no overall development plan at the time of writing, although an entire block opposite has been demolished. So I will not take you into these realms. Instead, after Wyndham's Theatre, come down an alley between it and Leicester Square Tube Station. It is part of St Martin's Court and was much connected with my stagestruck youth which ran concurrently with the bookish one. The stage doors of what is now the Albery (then the New) Theatre and Wyndham's face each other and, next to the Albery, are the large double doors for moving scenery in and out. When they were open my eager, teenage eyes looked down upon the actual stage. There was, also, the good chance of seeing real actors and actresses going in or out of the two theatres. Now there is an unromantic overhead passage in corrugated ferro-concrete between the two playhouses which are still, however, under the same management, that of the Albery family. The name of the New was changed in 1973, which was fitting because Sir Bronson Albery, grandfather of the present manager, was the stepson of Sir Charles Wyndham for whom it was built in 1903. In the days when its gallery was a series of inadequately upholstered benches without backs I spent hours waiting for admission, having 'put down a stool' to establish my rights to a gallery seat at a cost of 3d., paid to a bronchial, red-nosed woman who made as small a living from her trade as the buskers, who entertained us while we were waiting, did from theirs. Both are now victims of redundancy because all seats are bookable. Ironically, the theatres today are very rarely full, as they were when we sat like sardines in the New Theatre gallery to watch Richardson as Falstaff and Olivier as Oedipus.

At the end of St Martin's Court, on the right, is the Salisbury, a pub famous for its cut-glass mirrors. It is overdecorated in an amusingly opulent style and has shallow alcoves which afford some privacy.

At the Albery turn left into the Lane again. Beyond the theatre are two restaurants widely – even wildly – different in character. Beotys is Greek-run, but at least in London Greek food is permitted to be served hot, and there is a wide range of other continental dishes. I haven't actually tasted the cuisine at the other where you are said to be able to 'Dine in Royal Style at the Court of Henry VIII', off traditional English fare at its finest. A continuous medieval pageantry is advertised and the menu (in 1983, note) offered Wolsey's Beef Casserole as main dish for £13.95, inclusive of mead.

There is a six-road junction just ahead. At approximately ten o'clock is Great Newport Street. It isn't Great at all; it's short but distinguished because on one side it has the Photographers' Gallery, plus bookshop and the Arts Theatre Club, plus restaurant. The Photographers' Gallery, whose Associate Director has illustrated this book, is assisted by the Arts Council of Great Britain which has offices and a bookshop in Long Acre (at two o'clock); we go into Garrick Street (at four o'clock) where the large anonymous building halfway down on the right is a haunt of my middle age.

It is the Garrick Club to which the great actor did not belong because, for one reason, he died before its foundation in 1831. However, as actors in his day were even less acceptable socially than they were when Henry Irving was blackballed in 1873, it is not certain that he would have passed muster. Today leading actors are members and have their portraits displayed on its walls which are adorned with the finest collection of theatrical paintings in the country. In the company of a member they may be seen, as may Garrick's chair from Drury Lane, the letter objecting to Irving's proposed membership, and other valued theatrical items. (There is a ridiculous convention in London that the names of clubs do not appear anywhere on their exteriors. This is because it is supposed that Gentlemen would always KNOW – or their coachmen would. There is little difficulty in locating the Garrick because there is nothing else in a short street which it could possibly be, but the stranger in Pall Mall has to be pitied. See Walk Seven.)

At the end of Garrick Street, on the left, up a passage, is a good pub, the Lamb and Flag, and on the right another, the Round House, where, on its first floor, I once attended meetings of the Playwrights' Club. At the Garrick there are dramatists who have not only written plays but had them performed in the West End; at the Round House, in the early 1950s, the clientèle was different. We had all written plays but they had not been performed *anywhere*. This seemed to me unfortunate, not to say frustrating, so I inaugurated a production group and we staged one member's play – not mine I should add. This enterprise was so bitterly resented by most members that the club was dissolved soon after. The Round House, happily, has had greater resilience, and is still there facing Moss Bros, where you can hire or buy evening wear.

There is a four-way junction here but not strictly a crossroads. Go into Bedford Street where, down on the left, is the entrance to Inigo Place leading to the church of St Paul's, Covent Garden, known as the Actors' Church, and renowned for its profane association with Shaw and *Pygmalion* as much as for its Christian attributes. Inigo Jones was commissioned by the Russell family to design the church for their new estate. He was told it should be no better than a barn, so he determined, as every architectural student knows, that it should be 'the most handsome barn in England'.

Jones had not only the Russells to contend with in building St Paul's but also Bishop Laud who insisted that the altar must be placed at the east end so that the architect's fine portico (background for the start of Shaw's play as for *My Fair Lady*) could not be the entrance, for all that it faced the piazza. So he built a lesser one at the west end which we approach through a pleasant garden backed on to by offices and a hospital. We enter a vestibule through, if you please, all-plate-glass doors, from which we go into a light, wide interior gloriously barnlike in its proportions. It appears wider than it is because there are no pillars.

The apparent stage associations as one looks around are mostly twentieth-century, but there are earlier ones. William Wycherley,

Restoration dramatist, was buried here in 1721, also, in 1797, the actor Charles Macklin at the alleged age of 97, although some said he was ten years older. William Schwenk Gilbert was baptized at St Paul's in 1837 and there are connections with the other arts. The baby Turner saw the font in 1775, Thomas Rowlandson and Sir Peter Lely were buried here, so was Grinling Gibbons. Showbiz looms larger as we come to the twentieth century. Ellen Terry's ashes are in a casket, Noel Coward has a panel. He was an avowed atheist, according to his diaries, but so probably were others whose names adorn this peaceful church. Perhaps the contribution made by most of us unbelievers is the material one which we place in the restoration-fund box to be found in every church and cathedral. How dull our cities and villages would be without spires and steeples and clock towers. And what a refreshing change is St Paul's, Covent Garden, which has monuments to men and women who entertained us, rather

The Piazza Covent Garden

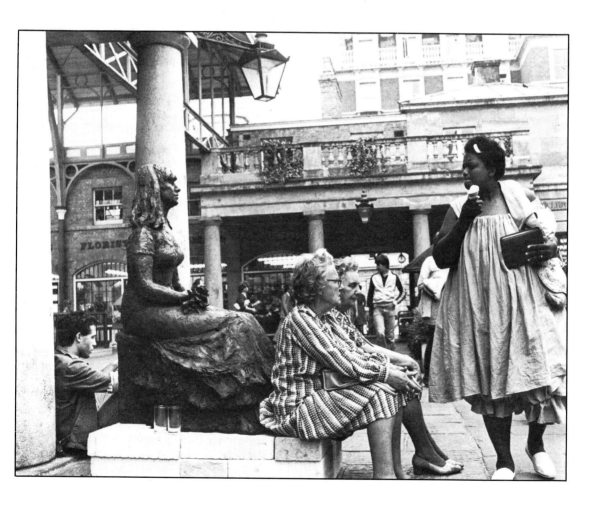

than to those who served the 'Em-pah'. None the less, it is still a Christian church with morning services on Sundays and it is open Monday–Friday, 9.30–4. It is popular for memorial services. Return to the garden and leave by a passage to King Street, coming out almost opposite The Grange, a restaurant where personal attention to both cuisine and clientèle is given priority. Use it for special occasions but you must book.

Covent Garden, only a few steps away, was a produce garden for Westminster Abbey in medieval times. The Russell family (which includes the Dukes of Bedford) bought it after the Reformation for high-class development. The centre was laid out as a piazza in the Italian style with classical and Renaissance-type buildings around it, and Bedford House facing south. Then the Russells decided to revive the market, which they were entitled to do, and this gradually took over. Bedford House was demolished, so was much of Inigo Jones's work, and in 1830 the third Duke of Bedford had the present market building erected. The date is given on the stonework at the east end. The Russells laid out much more of London in larger estates, especially in the Bloomsbury area, but they now own nothing of Covent Garden, which was sold in Edwardian times and the proceeds invested in, of all things, Tsarist bonds. The family retained only its right to a box in the opera house but even that went eventually, as the present Duke has recorded in his amusing memoirs.

Since the fruit and vegetable market was removed to Nine Elms, Battersea, in 1974, Covent Garden has been transformed totally in atmosphere but very little architecturally. At first, after the market went, it was a desolate area. The quiet was truly disturbing. The pubs clung to what passing trade there was; most of the warehouses and shops beneath the arcades were empty. Then plans to redevelop the site were rejected and it was decided to convert the vast central market building into a pedestrianized shopping area with stalls as well as shops. So the market returned under another guise and now operates both under the glassed-in and partly solid-roofed central area, and outside it, mostly in the open space adjoining Tavistock Street. The stalls have all the expected items of clothing, iron-mongery, household goods, confectionery plus those unusual items, antique or junk, which make markets exciting to prowl around. You can even buy fruit and veg. In the main building, which is in three parts with covered corridors between, and vaults below, you may purchase an assortment of goods and take a variety of refreshment. There are two bookshops: Hammick's which is general, and Penguin's where there is a bias towards that imprint. The shops are on three levels but they do not necessarily have the same owners at all of them.

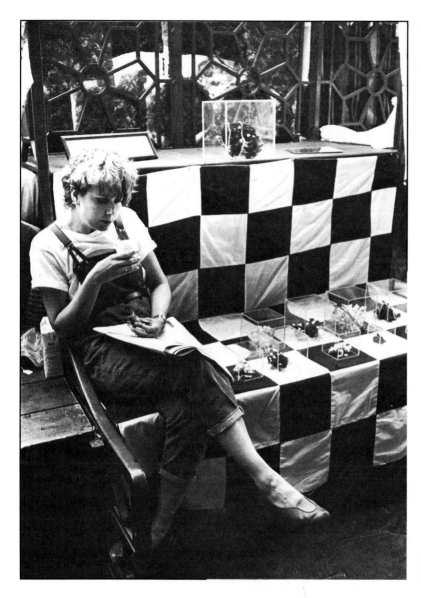

Stall holder
Covent Garden

The Crusting Pipe, on the lowest level, to which there are steps down into two courtyards, is a wine and steak bar. There are tables outside on the paving or inside in dim-lit caverns which appear romantic or sinister according to your outlook. The service is friendly and brisk and the house wine quite reasonably priced if you consider the rents and rates that traders here have to pay for smallish shops. (One of them reports his to be £30,000 p.a.) The Crusting Pipe specializes in fine and rare vintage ports which their handout claims are 'decanted

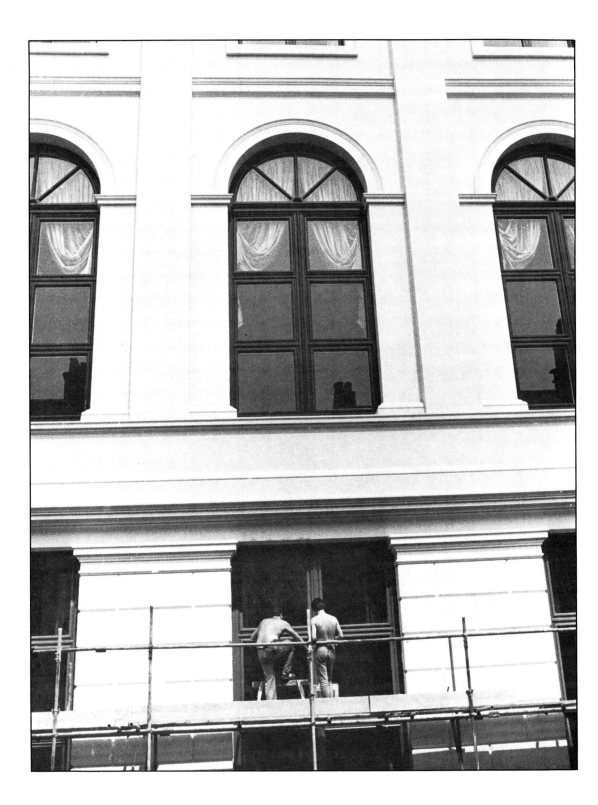

daily for gentlemen in the proper manner'. It is a most agreeable spot for a pre- or after-theatre drink and the courtyard is so sheltered that I have sat in it comfortably on a February evening. Alas, it is not open on Sundays, but the London Transport Museum, in what was the flower market building in the south corner of the piazza, is. It is laid out with all the expected contemporary skill and attention to detail. There are lots of visual aids but they are not needed for the larger exhibits which are actual buses, trams, trolleys, tube-train coaches, a working lift, and so on. It is immensely popular with children who flock to it in such numbers that there must be a case for moving it to less cramped quarters. Note, on a wall plaque, La Compagnie Général des Omnibus de Londres, Established in Paris in 1855. This was a precursor of the London General Omnibus Company, which originally had its offices in the French capital where the first omnibus ran in 1820.

It opens daily 10–6, except Christmas and Boxing Day; there is a charge for admission. On leaving you may pay also for a ride on a vintage bus (motor, not horse) to Charing Cross, Piccadilly and Oxford Street.

The piazza has ample space at each end for buskers, pop groups and other entertainers. Also, once a year, it becomes a temporary car-park for the mostly vintage automobiles which drive in from Burgundy loaded with Beaujolais Nouveau. Leave by the eastern end, noting the Italianate Floral Hall on your left. This glass and iron construction, reminiscent of the Great Exhibition of 1851, was badly damaged by a fire in 1956. It now stores scenery for the opera house which looms up behind it. The gardens beside the Floral Hall end in a *trompe-l'œil* wall on a house in which a man is walking at first-floor level, *à la* Magritte, towards us. The sculpture in the garden is called Man Rock and is by Antony Gormley. Approach it walking towards the wall and it depicts a person clinging to the breast of another creature, or perhaps to Mother Earth. The outline of the person is emphasized, enhanced even, by the algae which have grown on it. Against the painted wall, with its drawn-in *cupressi*, are real silver birches.

Turn left out of Russell Street into Bow Street, which is no longer strewn with cabbage leaves and banana skins, nor are there porters carrying a dozen baskets of produce upon their heads any more. But the police are still here at Bow Street Station and Magistrates' Court where they also have a small museum which gives the history of the force and of its precursors, the Bow Street Runners. And so is the Opera House, a fine enough building if it were better sited and if what should be a balcony above the lofty entrance hall had not been turned

Opera House extension
Covent Garden (opposite)

into the Crush Bar. The back of the bar presses against the columns of the frontage making it appear that the builders are in and have erected a temporary cabin in which to pore over plans and brew tea. High above it is a frieze in which there is much sculpted activity, but it badly needs cleaning.

There have been three theatres on this site. The present one is mid-Victorian, dating from 1858. Its predecessors were burned down, the usual fate of theatres until this century when they have suffered bombing instead. The conflagration which destroyed the first early-eighteenth-century playhouse in 1808 cost the lives of twenty-three firefighters. Its replacement, modelled on a Greek temple, lasted less than half a century and saw the virtual end of Covent Garden as a theatre. After 1842 it became an opera house which, with intervals for pantomime, revue and even cinema, it has remained ever since. The auditorium is ornate and lush: there are tiers of boxes and glittering chandeliers and bewigged, powdered footmen hold open the rich red curtains for prima donnas to take their calls. Nowadays banks, insurance companies, international conglomerates and the Arts Council subsidize productions, but as each performance only increases the total cost each opera has a limited showing.

Continue up Bow Street to Long Acre where there is a smartly painted pub, Kemble's Head, on the corner (the Kembles were nineteenth-century actors). Turn right opposite an office development on what the ponderous Odhams Press building of the 1930s once stood. Its site became, for a few years, a sunken garden and open space cared for by the Friends of Covent Garden who hoped it would be scheduled to stay so. Alas, it and other nearby sites were too valuable to be allowed to remain unbuilt upon. This area of central London could do with more greenery, as is emphasized by the attempts made to adorn the new offices with window-boxes and trailing plants.

Continue along Long Acre. Facing you as you cross Drury Lane into Great Queen Street is a massive edifice which could be mistaken for a mausoleum to a whole dynasty of crowned heads. It is Freemasons' Hall which comprises offices, banqueting rooms and suites, and the headquarters of freemasonry in Britain. Pevsner calls it 'bewilderingly self-possessed' and refers to its 'corner erection', the tower. In this there appear to be four separate tombs, with two columns rising above each of them, to the pediment, which surely ought to have a giant statue crowning it? Instead it ends in a flat plinth. Far below is a curiously kitsch electric clock over the great studded double doors from which you expect someone like Agamemnon to emerge at any moment. The hall is only about fifty years old and survived the war. Indeed, you can imagine the bombs bouncing off it. Follow its great hulk down Wild Street (to the right) in the general direction of the river. When at last it ends there is a simple board school cowering beneath it, and then another later monster, Space House, a round essay in concrete which is at least easier on the eye than a glass box. Turn right into Kemble Street and re-cross Drury Lane with the colonnaded side of the Theatre Royal on your left.

A much, much smaller playhouse, the Fortune, faces its stage door. The exterior (1924) is said to resemble the seventeenth-century City theatre of the same name but you could be forgiven for not realizing this as you look at its stuccoed frontage with a naked goddess looking down benevolently from the region of the upper circle. Its interior is too steeply raked for comfort but it has its place in theatrical history because it was here in 1961 that four young Oxbridge graduates brought about an irrevocable, not to say irreverent, change in the nature of intimate revue with their hilarious Edinburgh Festival Show, *Beyond the Fringe*. Jonathan Miller, Peter Cook, Alan Bennett and Dudley Moore did not become globally as famous as another young quartet from Liverpool who burst upon the world at about the same time, but to squares like me they were more acceptable. It is sobering to reflect that, under present Equity ruling, *Beyond the Fringe* could probably not open in the West End because the four performers would not have appeared for the statutory number of weeks as paid actors in the provinces.

Follow the Theatre Royal as you turn left into Catherine Street. In the eighteenth and nineteenth centuries Drury Lane and Covent Garden vied with each other as the major London theatres. Here Garrick and Macready reigned, and Edmund Kean, whose performances Coleridge likened to 'reading Shakespeare by flashes of lightning'. Pepys described the first theatre which opened in 1663 at the beginning of the Restoration. It was mostly destroyed by fire nine years later. Its successor went up in flames in 1809 and this gave rise to an anecdote almost as famous as the architectural one about the barn. The lessee was Richard Brinsley Sheridan, dramatist and member of Parliament. He is alleged to have watched the blaze from a nearby coffee-house. When his composure was commented upon he remarked, 'surely a man may enjoy a drink by his own fireside'. The auditorium was rebuilt in the 1920s and the Theatre Royal Drury Lane has become the leading home of the musical, with *Oklahoma!*, *My Fair Lady* and other hit shows having their London premières here. The frontage is heavy and uninteresting but inside it is good red plush with boxes around the back of the grand circle as well as along its sides. There is an inner domed foyer with statues of Garrick and Kean in niches, and the circle bar with an alcoved end is I swear larger than some council flats. On one occasion I ordered a bottle of wine for the interval and carried it to our box (a box is cheaper than four grand circle seats), whereupon a flunkey popped his head over the front and said, 'GLC regulations, sir. No drinking in the auditorium.' Before I could protest too strongly he added, 'I will give you a private room', and led us down side corridors to a chamber by the pass door to back stage. In it was a *chaise-longue*, several chairs and an upright piano. Officials in evening dress came through the pass door and saluted us politely. As the interval drew to a close the flunkey reappeared and led us by 'the quick way' back to our box.

Catherine Street leads into the Aldwych which forms a crescent with part of the Strand. Aldwych means 'an old outlying farm', which is not easy to imagine as you turn left and pass the Waldorf Hotel (plaque to Ivor Novello, who lived and died in a flat near its roof, and who was part of Drury Lane's history) and then the Aldwych Theatre. Here there ought to be a plaque to Charles Dickens, although he has at least seven already, not because he lived in a house or drank in a pub on this site but because more than a century after his death he achieved new success as a playwright with the Royal Shakespeare Company's adaptation of *Nicholas Nickleby* which lasted for nearly nine hours over two nights, and showed the genius of our theatre at its finest.

At Kingsway cross to Bush House which has, written into its stonework, the words 'To the Friendship of English Speaking Peoples'. It was built between the wars, long after the area had been cleared of slums to make Kingsway, by American architects, and is a complex of high buildings with courtyards and sliproads. A centrepiece, facing up Kingsway, is joined to them by colonnades and steps to the Strand. In their guide to *The Architecture of London*, Edward Jones and Christopher Woodward refer to Bush House's 'vulgar but grand exedra and the heap of masonry on top of it which bring a welcome flourish of American Corinthian to London'. Pevsner tells us that the exedra is an 'entrance niche' which his glossary defines as 'the apsidal end of a room'. The niche in this case (also an 'exit niche') is most imposing and leads to a whole building. The slogan quoted above it is explicable only as a manifestation of Anglo-American solidarity although, properly, it should embrace India House, Australia House (both inside the crescent) and certainly the offices and studios of the External Broadcasting Department of the BBC whose influence is so lamentably underrated by the present government.

Bush House, Aldwych
The Exedra
(opposite)

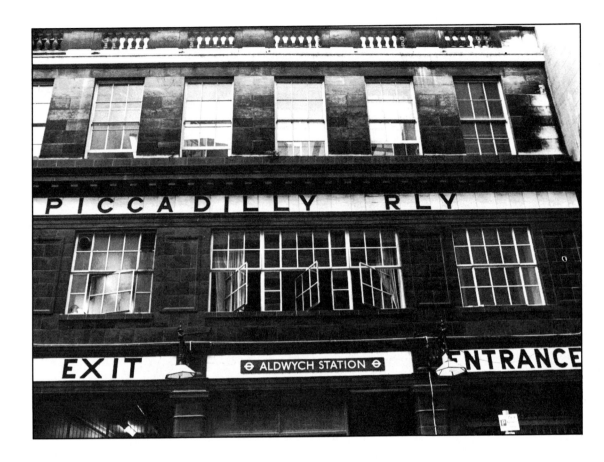

London Transport Aldwych Station

At the end of my National Service with the RAF I spent several months in an Air Ministry office in Bush House where there was a department planning the post-war air works. My most vivid memory is of genial senior officers passing their days making paper aircraft and seeing how far up Kingsway they could make them fly.

Proceed to the east end of Aldwych for a fine view of the church of St Clement Danes isolated in mid thoroughfare behind a statue to William Gladstone. The name may or may not have a connection with Alfred the Great permitting repulsed Danish invaders who had married English wives to settle in the district (laws about immigrants are nothing new), but St Clement is certainly the patron saint of sailors. There was a timber-framed church here well over a thousand years ago, when there might well have also been an 'aldwych'. The wooden building was replaced by others including the one which escaped in 1666, only to be demolished by Wren who was never so busy that he couldn't take on yet another task. His tower was added to by James Gibbs and survived the fire of 1941 when the main building was gutted. It stayed a ruin until 1955 when it was restored as the central church of the RAF (is there a patron saint of airmen?). It has a grand wide central aisle and a high balcony on pillars. It is now in the same parish as St Mary-le-Strand which is on another island round which the traffic throbs to Charing Cross and Waterloo. An earlier church was taken down by the Duke of Somerset because it lay in the path of his new mansion (see below), and James Gibbs was commissioned to design the present one under an act of Queen Anne's reign calling for fifty new places of worship. A placard appealing for funds states that in Sir John Betjeman's estimation, it is 'a baroque paradise'. It has a handsome three-tier tower above a clockface looking westward along the Strand, almost but not quite on a line with Gibbs's St Martin-in-the-Fields, and it is a pity that the traffic cannot be barred from one side of it to make it easier to visit. On its Thames-side lies Somerset House, the vast neo-classical mansion on the site of the one which brought about the demolition of the church. Seen from the south bank it is a magnificent pile, and so it is with its wide frontage on the river, its courtyards and gatehouse, its beautifully proportioned rooms and its galleries rising from the Embankment. All this splendour went into purpose-built government

Somerset House

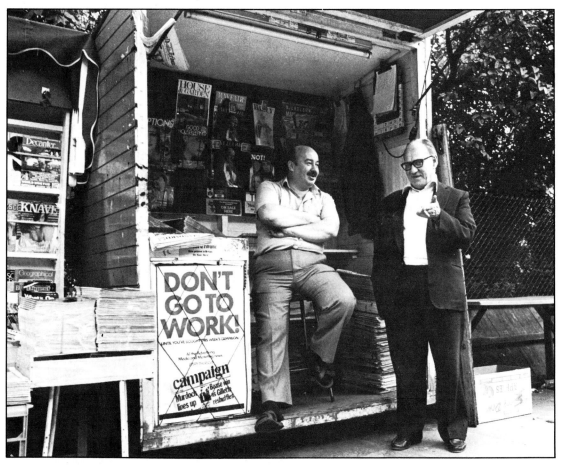

Newsstand Temple Station
To be seen from
Waterloo Bridge

offices which became the registry of our births, deaths and marriages. What a waste! These records have now been removed and discussion has since raged on the proper use to which the building should be put. For a while it seemed possible that it would become the permanent home of Turner's pictures but the Trustees of the Tate rejected this. Next to it, on the City side, is King's College, part of the University of London, a dark grey sombre mass from the outside but within can be seen pleasant courts and terraces.

Continue westwards to Waterloo Bridge and walk across it, having first passed by a lot more of implacably anonymous Somerset House. From the bridge, which was officially opened in 1945, having contrived to get itself rebuilt, particularly during World War Two, to the design of Sir Giles Gilbert Scott, there are incomparable vistas which never fail to delight me. I do not remember the original early nineteenth-century bridge, nor the view from it, but its opening was recorded by Constable and it was painted also by Monet.

As one looks east and west there are too many tower blocks but there is much to please the eye at all levels. By the river children (the modern mudlarks) scavenge, on it barges are moored and pleasure boats throb by. St Paul's still stands out clearly (as do the Barbican and NatWest tower), but the wedding-cake spire of St Bride's (see Walk Two) is obscured by contemporary structures.

Surprisingly, perhaps, we are once more in theatreland because facing us, on the south bank, is the concrete complex of that bleak architectural misfortune, the National Theatre, designed by Sir Denys Lasdun. It has terraces which face the river, spacious foyers, restaurants, bars, an underground car-park. Its dressing-rooms, wardrobe, scene docks and rehearsal area are all that a national theatre should have. My quarrel is with its auditoria (there are three) and its unprepossessing exterior. Until this century architects took care about detail. Sometimes there was too much of it and one yearned for simplicity but now it is apparently in order to leave gaps between layers of pre-stressed concrete, or, as here, to allow bulky fly-towers to ascend sixty or seventy feet unadorned, to gild the lily scarcely at all. This is particularly unfortunate here because part of the art of the theatre is concerned with papering over the cracks, making insubstantial scenery appear solid masonry. This we still get in actual productions within the three theatres but not outside in the over-elaborate areas which Alastair Service calls 'an extension of the spaces of the theatre into the everyday world'. But I don't want those spaces to penetrate my world. I wish to submit to the suspension of disbelief on which all fiction, on printed page, stage and screen, depends. It says much for the greatness of our tradition that in all three theatres I have seen plays where the actors and directors have overcome the shortcomings of their environment to superb effect, or, to be fair, used it to aid their performances.

The three theatres are called the Olivier, the Lyttelton and the Cottesloe. Oliver Lyttelton was Chairman of the National Theatre Board, Laurence Olivier was its first director when it was at the Old Vic, and Lord Cottesloe was Chairman of the body responsible to the government for building the NT. With due respect to Lyttelton and Cottesloe, the theatres named after them should have been called by theatrical names. Shaw would have been appropriate, or Granville-Barker, since they led the early campaigns for a national home for drama, and their plays are acted still.

But we now have a national theatre and it does fine work. Tours of it are organized on most days for a small fee. (You can reserve tickets.) These take you into all three auditoria but backstage only at the Lyttelton and the Cottesloe. When I went on one an enthusiastic young man assured me that you can see and hear from all seats in all three: I know you can't, but I admired his spirited defence of the NT for which he obviously was proud to work. Over 700 people are employed behind the scenes or front of house at the NT, and most of those encountered share this pride, from the smiling ushers and usherettes to the man who bids you a cheerful good-night as he takes your car-parking fee. The bars and restaurants are open all day and not restricted to playgoers, musicians are usually playing informally in the foyers and my only complaint about the front-of-house organization is the filthy wine which is sold. (I now take my own in a thermos and that is against the regulations.)

Another feature calling for comment is security. Michael Flanders and Donald Swann once had a song in which they guyed the LCC regulations for running theatres. The exit doors, they sang, must be opened at the end of each performance, the safety curtain must be lowered during the course of the show. This could not be applied to the National where the doors operate on the swing principle and are never fastened back, and in the Olivier with its open stage there is no safety curtain. Nor did I discern one on my backstage tour of the Cottesloe. Yet in the latter such is the concern for safety that the one meagre bar has no shelves on which interval drinks could be placed. These, apparently, would be a fire hazard. It is a wonder the performances are allowed at all when you think of the potential dangers from those gantries of lighting equipment.

As you cross under Waterloo Bridge into the continuing concrete jungle, spare a thought for the Old Vic Theatre, five minutes' down the road. That is where my generation, and several which preceded it, had their greatest theatrical experiences. That is where the National started, taking over from the Old Vic Trust which carried on the work of the remarkable Lilian Baylis. She turned a music hall into a theatre dedicated to presenting Shakespeare and the classics at prices anyone could afford. Happily, the theatre has now reopened under new management and it is possible to sit again in its plushy Victorian interior.

The NT buildings are connected to those on the other side of the bridge at two levels. Stay by the river and note, literally beneath the arches, the National Film Theatre. Then comes a somewhat confusing amalgam of halls and galleries linked by steps, ramps, courts and catwalks not as simply signposted as they might be. It is all, roughly, on the site of what was the Festival of Britain in 1951, a joyous expression of what life could or should be like, which marked the beginning of the end of wartime austerity. It was planned by the much-maligned Attlee Labour administration and was an important

showpiece of contemporary design, as well as being a celebration of our national achievements, characteristics and foibles. The present complex of buildings is less a matter for congratulation apart from the Festival Hall, the only surviving relic which is exciting inside and out. There has been an extension to it on the river side which slightly spoils the original effect of the apparently suspended concert hall seen through the windows of the entrance. Skilful use of glass and stairways gives a first impression of a huge floating mass. Inside it is equally satisfactory and moderately conventional, more like a cinema than a theatre, with broken tiers of boxes on either side projecting from the walls rather than sunk into them. Although primarily intended for orchestral concerts it can also be adapted for stage performances of dancing, including full ballets. Because I like to tap my feet and wave my arms I do not go much to concerts, so my experience of it as a place in which to listen to music is limited. My neighbour, a conductor, thinks highly of it as a performer, so take the advice of the professional arm-waver.

The Festival Hall has certainly become an integral part of London's musical life over three decades, as have the smaller Queen Elizabeth Hall and the Purcell Room, which is used mainly for recitals. Behind and to one side of them stands the Hayward Gallery whose peculiar

Queen Elizabeth Hall
and
Royal Festival Hall

chunky shape defies definition. It is something of a fantasy building such as a child might produce with a large bag of assorted-sized bricks. When you run out of one set you improvise with another. Once again the finishing is crude but there is nothing in the decoration to distract one from the pictures. There is no permanent exhibition apart from the strange metal construction on one roof. It lights up and twists round according to the direction and strength of the wind and does undoubtedly add some brightness at night. But more natural colour is needed over the whole complex, which suffers further drabness from the enormous Shell Centre dominating the skyline towards Waterloo Station. Inside it over five thousand workers are said to be employed. It is a terrible monument to the planning failures of the 1950s and 1960s.

You can go to the north bank via Hungerford Footbridge but I suggest that instead you go by Waterloo Bridge, the pleasing simplicity of which can be admired from the Queen's Walk. On your way you may observe an object called Zemran, by William Pye. It was presented to the GLC in 1972 by Nadia Nerina, and looks as though it has escaped from a boiler-room.

Once on the bridge again pause to take in the panorama and pick out the Palace of Westminster, the Abbey, the domed roof of Methodist Central Hall, and the joys of Whitehall Court, a Victorian extravaganza of a building, all spires, pinnacles, balconies, bays, bows and every architectural conceit imaginable ('enough to make Chambord pale with envy', says Pevsner). We pass close to it on Walk Four but it is better seen from afar, from here on Waterloo Bridge, or across St James's Park. It houses the National Liberal Club and many apartments.

Nelson eventually heaves into view, about mid river, having been lost against the enormity of New Zealand House. Closer at hand are the implacable Shell-Mex House, rising behind Embankment Gardens, apparently encased indefinitely in plaster of Paris against permanent multiple fractures, and the less severe Savoy Hotel beside it. Shell-Mex House was once the Cecil Hotel, with a different river frontage. It has been part of the riverscape for so long that one would feel a loss without it. Shall we ever feel that about the same international company's south-bank skyscraper? To be fair, we might.

At the end of Waterloo Bridge, after passing a shirtmaker 'By Appointment to the Queen', turn left into the Strand, an undistinguished, traffic-rent street in which you pass the front of the Savoy Hotel, set back down a very necessary drive-in for cabs. Tucked beneath and beside it on the steep slope to the Embankment is the Savoy Theatre where most of the Gilbert and Sullivan light operas were first presented. It was actually there before the hotel was built and was the first theatre in the world to be lit by electricity. The original bulbs must still be in use: when I was last in its stalls the light was so dim I couldn't read the programme.

Roughly opposite the Savoy Hotel, where the rich stay and eat in its famous grill-room, is the Strand Palace Hotel which is for the less affluent, who also attend 'functions'. No London hotel is complete without its Functions Room for trade association dinners, old boys' reunions, retirement luncheons, anniversary parties, etc. They are also held at the Savoy but there they are called receptions, banquets, even soirées.

Gilbert & Sullivan pub opposite the Savoy

We turn left off the Strand at Villiers Street immediately before a third hotel, behind which is Charing Cross Station. On its first floor, up a marbled staircase, is a high-ceilinged, gracious dining-room in which British Rail serves polite English afternoon teas. My younger daughter chose it for childhood birthday celebrations. The hotel makes a handsome entrance to the station, in the forecourt of which stands a replica of the Eleanor Cross mentioned in Walk Three.

Facade in Adam Street

Opposite are the famous Nash 'pepperpots' still standing at the ends of what was West Strand Improvements, on a triangular site. Between them Nash designed handsome terraces of which only some of the façades are extant. They were first spoiled long ago when a central arcade (itself not part of the original conception) was removed to make way for Coutts Bank, in 1903. That was bad enough but recently Coutts had all the buildings gutted and replaced their own with a starkly contemporary glass structure which is totally out of keeping with the Nash frontage. What is the point of the law requiring planning permission for almost every construction from a garden shed to a towerblock when this kind of outrage is condoned? It might have been better if the whole site had been razed and the pepperpots sent to the V&A.

Villiers Street is seedy and leads to Embankment Underground Station and the Embankment Gardens. Off to the left are the remains of the Adam Brothers' estate, once dominated by the Adelphi, their gracious masterpiece overlooking the Thames. The planners of the 1930s permitted this to be demolished in favour of a hideous office block which, alas, was not removed by Hitler's bombs. Surrounding it are Robert, Buckingham and John Adam Streets, with some of the elegant terrace houses which the brothers designed, but too many have gone. Off to the right of Villiers Street are the Arches where lovers and beggars lurk, where there are wine vaults, and the Players' Theatre Club, dedicated to keeping alive the songs and monologues of the old music-hall.

The walk ends in Embankment Gardens where there is an outdoor café, a bandstand, well-tended flower beds, ponds, trees and the actual Watergate used by the Duke of Buckingham when the river was more of a highway for local journeys than it now is. There is statuary to be inspected before resting on one of the many seats. Sir Arthur Sullivan (bust only) faces the Savoy Theatre with a distraught lady in flowing garments falling against the plinth. Robert Burns, sober and alert, sits on a stone tree-stump with books at his feet. Robert Raikes, founder of Sunday schools, has a monument curiously unvandalized by the children whom he committed to so much tedium. There are also seats on the actual Embankment, overlooking the river. Cleopatra's Needle stands near by, covered in characters depicting wondrous deeds done in Ancient Egypt, and guarded by sphinxes. This item of pink granite dates back to about 1500 BC and bears no relevance whatever to London's history. It was a gift from the Turkish ruler of Egypt in 1819. It weighs 180 tons and for complicated reasons took nearly seventy years to arrive here. New York in its Central Park boasts a twin.

Walk Six

Trafalgar Square – National Portrait Gallery –
Leicester Square – Soho – Fitzrovia – University of London –
The Courtauld – The Brunswick Centre – Doughty Street –
Gray's Inn – Bloomsbury Square – The British Museum –
Russell Square

British Museum

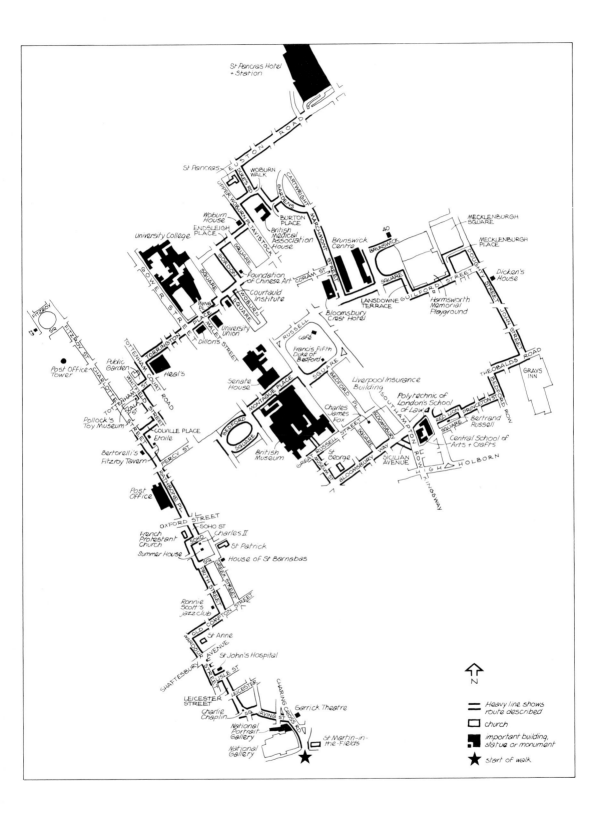

St Pancras Hotel
+ Station

St Pancras

WOBURN
WALK

MECKLENBURGH
SQUARE

MECKLENBURGH
PLACE

Woburn
House

ENDSLEIGH
PLACE

BURTON
PLACE

British
Medical
Association
House

Brunswick
Centre

40

Dicken's
House

University College

Foundation
of Chinese Art

Courtauld
Institute

LANSDOWNE
TERRACE

Harmsworth
Memorial
Playground

Byng
PLACE

University
Union

Dillon's Street

Bloomsbury
Crest Hotel

Café

Francis Fifth
Duke of
Bedford

THEOBALDS   ROAD

GRAYS
INN

FITZROY
SQ

Public
Garden

Heal's

Post Office
Tower

Senate
House

Liverpool Insurance
Building

Polytechnic of
London's School
of Law

Central School of
Arts + Crafts

Pollock's
Toy Museum

COLVILLE PLACE
Etoile

Charles
James
Fox

RED LION
SQUARE

Bertrand
Russell

HOLBORN

Bertorelli's
Fitzroy Tavern

PERCY ST

British
Museum

St
George

SICILIAN
AVENUE

KINGSWAY

Post
Office

OXFORD   STREET

SOHO ST

French
Protestant
Church

Charles II

St Patrick

Summer
House

House of St Barnabas

Ronnie
Scott's
Jazz club

St Anne

St John's Hospital

SHAFTESBURY   AVENUE

LEICESTER
STREET

Charlie
Chaplin

Garrick Theatre

National
Portrait
Gallery

St Martin-in-
the-Fields

National
Gallery

N

═ Heavy line shows
route described

☐ church

■ important building,
statue or monument

★ start of walk

Leave the square opposite the front of St Martin's and walk a few yards up by the side of the National Gallery until you come to the entrance to the National Portrait Gallery. There may well be an artist – his work not represented in either – drawing in coloured chalks on the paving stones. Having assessed the quality of his work, and rewarded him accordingly, enter the NPG where you are advised to start your visit on the second floor and work downwards. This is because the most modern portraits are on the ground floor. Why, I don't know, unless the curator thinks it more likely that to cater for what must be an ever-growing collection a basement will be added rather than an attic.

This admirable gallery founded in 1856 and moved here forty years later, is bursting its seams and more space will soon have to be found for it. It is comprised of paintings, drawings and photographs in its permanent rooms, but the living, apart from royalty, are not represented. Special exhibitions are mounted regularly and it is a measure of the lack of official stuffiness that for a few weeks in the 1970s a room was devoted to Osbert Lancaster's *The Littlehampton Bequest*, portraits, in pastiche of the great masters, of his cartoon characters.

The permanent collection is interesting more for its subjects than its artists, although there is work by most of the leading English portraitists. But the point of the gallery is to show what our great men and women looked like and a visit here is a recommended introduction to reading the history of Britain. There is an excellent catalogue and I mention only a few of the pictures and photographs which appeal to me. Not caring for lifts I ignore official advice and ascend the first stairs in sight to a landing where the First World War poets and generals are commemorated. There are photographs of Wilfred Owen, whose *Futility* is quoted in full, Siegfried Sassoon and Rupert Brooke, and a self-portrait by Isaac Rosenberg. Larger than any of them is Thomas Sargent's *Officers of the First World War*, a group painting of leading generals and field marshals mostly standing about casually, apart from the blimpish Baron Plumer. He is two away from Haig, who has a mystic look in his eyes. Or is he sleepwalking and counting corpses?

It is better yet to start at the top and move through the Tudors and Stuarts to the Georges, rather than ascending like a time machine in reverse, although it is the first floor which I find most interesting, with such pictures as Hayter's *Reformed House of Commons* of 1833. He took ten years to paint this scene of the chamber with the gallery overflowing, the clerks writing away industriously and the great crush of members, some listening, some talking. There is another of the

Shakespeare in Leicester Square (opposite)

collapse of Chatham in the House of Lords, and of the Commons again, before the fire of 1834, with clouds and trees visible beyond the arched windows at the end of the chamber. And there is a statue of Victoria and Albert as ancient Saxons. She looks up at him adoringly with her right hand on his left shoulder. He turns to her questioningly, with right arm half raised and index finger pointing upwards. Why, is open to surmise or even ribald comment.

Many of the lower rooms have themes such as 'The Struggle for America', 'Science and the Industrial Revolution', 'Poverty and the People', 'The Romantic Movement'. A feature of the Gallery is that portraits are not left in isolation to tell the whole story. They are supported by political caricatures, contemporary documents, silhouettes, engravings and books, and even by items of machinery. Painting relates to literature, architecture and music: all four are commentaries on life. Life embraces science, art, nature, and the displays emphasize the correlation between them. The only drawback I have to record is that too many of the exhibits are behind glass so that it is difficult, sometimes impossible, to view them without seeing reflections. This has been noted elsewhere and it is a constantly aggravating factor in visiting museums and galleries, even though John Ruskin delivered the opinion that paintings need the protection of glass. It could be that modern technology has outdated this view but if it hasn't it is better that we should bear with our own reflections than that future generations should not see the paintings at all.

Turn left on leaving the gallery and follow the curve of Charing Cross Road to the Irving statue and street of the same name. Henry Irving was the first actor to be knighted – in 1895 by Queen Victoria. The accolade conferred respectability on the profession at last but although there have been many stage knights since, Irving alone has a statue. For a few years he was also remembered in a club theatre in Irving Street, a small hall with a smaller stage which enjoyed brief popularity as a home of intimate revue. It could hardly have been less appropriately named because Irving was master of the large effect, a big actor who needed to play to a gallery. The playhouse opposite in Charing Cross Road named after Garrick would have been more suitable but Irving was still alive when it was opened. The Garrick, late Victorian, is neatly fitted in between larger buildings on the bend of the road, with its auditorium running alongside instead of behind the frontage. At circle level it has six columns on a balcony from which plants trail. Above it are a jolly frieze and six little eye windows beneath a balustrade.

Irving Street leads into Leicester Square and is mostly restaurants. The Square, first laid out in 1670 below the Earl of Leicester's house (long since demolished), is undistinguished. There has been no attempt to give it architectural cohesion and although there are lots of trees the flower beds are municipally formal. Also that scourge the pigeon has been permitted to take over. I wouldn't think of sitting on one of the many benches, but those who work near by and seek a lunchtime in the open air have little choice. Shakespeare has none. There he has been, since 1874, leaning elegantly on a book and covered with droppings. The so-called Baron Grant, a confidence trickster who nevertheless gave the gardens to the public, caused him

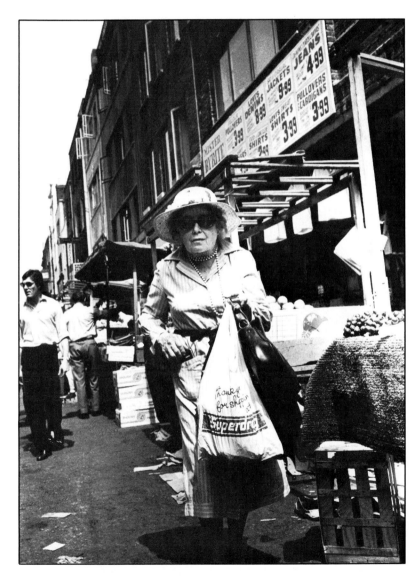

Berwick Market in the sleazy, Not Recommended part of Soho

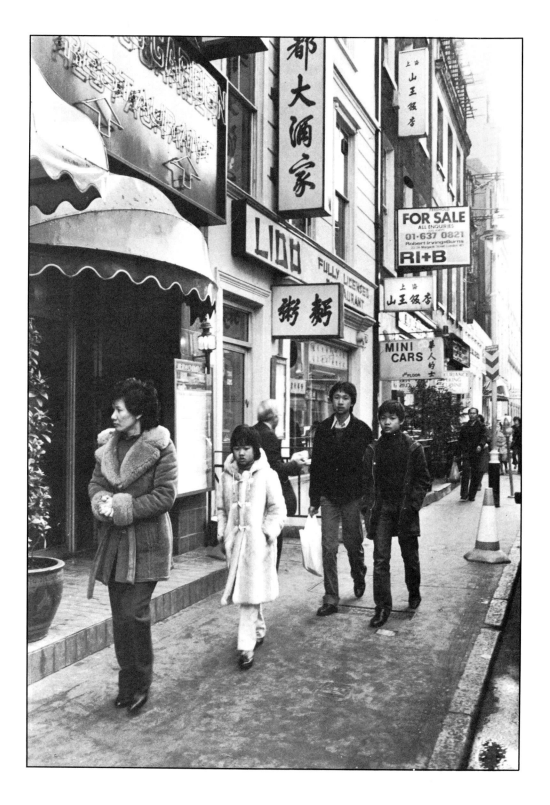

to be placed here. Other statues are to William Hogarth, Joshua Reynolds (both in rakish headgear), Isaac Newton and the surgeon John Hunter. They are all within the gardens. Outside, on the south west edge, is Charlie Chaplin, seen, in bronze, as the 'little fellow'. It is better not to look at the surrounding buildings although you can hardly fail to be aware of menacing megalometroland structures darkening the skyline. Major film premières and royal command performances happen here in glittering unreality. Leave by Leicester Street, roughly marking the site of the Earl's house. Facing its northern end is the pleasant, pointed, Dutch-style St John's Hospital for Skin Diseases. Turn left into Lisle Street, then right into Wardour Street. You are now in a miniature Chinatown with restaurants and takeaways on all sides. At Chinese New Year the little streets have a carnival atmosphere.

Cross Shaftesbury Avenue, still in Wardour Street, and soon, on the right, is the tower of St Anne's, Soho. The church was bombed in 1940 and the space where it stood is now a car-park. (Astonishing that after nearly half a century some streets still show their war scars.) On the Wardour Street side is a raised garden with benches and silver birches. Dorothy Sayers, who dramatized the life of Christ, and created Lord Peter Wimsey, was a churchwarden here. She is buried beneath the tower which also commemorates in tablets the essayist William Hazlitt and one Theodore, who was king of Corsica for a month in 1736. Verses by Horace Walpole record the latter's unfortunate career which ended in a debtor's prison.

You are now in Soho, parts of which are very sleazy indeed. Unless you have a taste for striptease and porn films I wouldn't advise you to linger in its mostly narrow streets and alleys, and certainly not at night. I don't wish to exaggerate its reputation but it is a district harbouring low-life night clubs, brothels and criminals' hideouts, although on its fringes there are many excellent restaurants, some of which we will pass as we go right along Old Compton Street, then left into Frith Street (where Ronnie Scott's jazz club is) or Greek Street to take us to Soho Square.

The origin of the name is not proved but a popular theory is that it derives from an old hunting cry – So-HO!, as in Tally-HO!, but it is a long time since anyone rode to hounds around here. It has always attracted immigrants ranging from French protestants on the run to Californian drop-outs, and this is reflected in the nationalities of the restaurants, and in the churches of Soho Square. On the north side is the French Protestant Church in a building which looks more like a merchant's town house; on the east is St Patrick's which could hardly be more Italianate inside or out, and is, of course, Roman Catholic. Although the building in

Soho's Chinatown Wardour St (opposite)

Soho Newsstand

which the French protestants worship dates from only 1893 their church was founded in 1550 when Edward VI gave a charter to Huguenot refugees, French and Dutch, led by a Polish minister. The congregation met in the City and elsewhere before settling here.

Soho Square is on the site of Monmouth House, the mansion of another nobleman (this one an illegitimate Son of Charles II), and dates from the late seventeenth century. The buildings on all sides are of various periods and the finest of them is undoubtedly the House of St Barnabas, a well-preserved mid-eighteenth-century town house, on the corner of Greek Street. It has attractive ceilings, wrought iron and plasterwork and may be inspected on Wednesday afternoons and Thursday mornings only.

In mid square is a mock Tudor summerhouse and on one of the paths a statue to Charles II. This was once part of a much larger monument with figures representing English rivers, which suggests it was inspired by Bernini's work in the Piazza Navona in Rome but there's no way of telling without a visit to Grimsdyke in Harrow, a Norman Shaw house where these figures are now preserved.

Cross Oxford Street – and for my money that is what I always do but more of that in the next walk – to Rathbone Place, a yawn of a thoroughfare with much of its west side taken up by a post office building whose monotonous wall is relieved only by a built-in war memorial. You now become fully aware of the giant Post Office Tower, the base of which is near to Fitzroy Square. It is a fine achievement of engineering, 580 feet high and useful in transmitting messages around the world in a few seconds. It is also an ugly excrescence, a stalactite in glass and steel lacking anything of the ecstatic beauty of a spire. The restaurant near its top, which revolved slowly to give diners a panoramic view, had to be closed because of bomb scares. The tower heaves into sight almost everywhere you walk in London and I cannot think how we shall ever be relieved of it in an acceptable way.

Rathbone Place leads into Charlotte Street which is great eating country with many excellent restaurants on either side and in adjacent Percy Street. Bertorelli's, rambling above and behind its street entrance, is friendly in an extravert Italian style; Au Savarin and L'Etoile are traditionally French with all the mouth-watering qualities that implies; Schmidt's, alas, Temple of the best of Wurst, and more rambling even than Bert's, has gone, and in Percy Street is the White Tower to which I go only when I am taken by a rich publisher. For serious drinkers there is the Fitzroy Tavern, once a favourite rendezvous for Dylan Thomas and other poets.

Charlotte Street becomes Fitzroy Street, and leads to Fitzroy Square. This latter has to be mentioned because at No. 29 the Bloomsbury Group may be said to have come into being. Virginia Stephen (later Woolf) and her brother Adrian moved into a house in which Bernard Shaw had lived in 1907, and there entertained Leonard Woolf, Lytton Strachey, E. M. Forster and others whose lives have been thoroughly documented. We ought to look at it – the square has been much paved over and is attractive – but we won't because we have plenty of Bloomsbury to come on this walk. Instead, we will take the second turning right after Percy Street into Colville Place, a quiet terrace facing a car-park which, in 1983, was vibrant with revolt behind its freshly-painted front doors. Banners flew from the frontages, bearing the message

GREEN FITZROVIA'S OPEN SPACE
NO OFFICE BLOCK IN COLVILLE PLACE.

The green was not visible amongst the parked vehicles. I suspect cockney irony.

Go left into Whitfield Street where, at No. 41, on the corner of Scala Street, is Pollock's Toy Museum, open on weekdays from 10 to 5, except bank holidays. You enter through a salesroom which is also the warehouse for the famous toy theatres that have been delighting children and their parents for a century and more. My favourite exhibit is of a painting of the Britannia, Hoxton, with four tiers of seats above the stalls. It was done by 'Mr Torrington, a frustrated artist apprenticed to the family business of umbrella making'. Mr Torrington, you deserved to earn your niche in posterity. The premises, on three floors of two houses converted into one, are very cramped and the kids must be kept in order. As well as theatrical exhibits there are dolls' houses, soldiers, teddy bears, board games and other toys. Note how small the rooms are. Living in a Georgian-style house was not necessarily an agreeable experience.

Turn left as you leave and bear right into Tottenham Street at the end of which, on the left, a bomb site has become a small public garden overlooked by a contemporary mural on the side of a house. This shows the people of Soho (all races and creeds) at work and play. Then cross Tottenham Court Road which is celebrated for its furniture stores, and especially for Heal's, which sells much else besides. Heal's has been in the forefront of 'contemporary' design for many generations and mounts eye-catching displays in its deep-set windows which merge with the sales floor. It is a joy to browse in and difficult to resist temptation in, although assistants can be hard to locate. I have several times been mistaken for one by those eager to make purchases. The east side of Tottenham Court Road has slightly more style than the west which is brash and much given over to video and recording technology.

After Heal's turn right into Torrington Place which crosses Gower Street. This is an area dominated by the University of London which began officially in 1836 when its charter was granted, but actually started in University College in the previous decade. UC was sponsored by private money to counteract the prevailing Anglican control of Oxford and Cambridge. Its founders were determinedly secular, it welcomed Jews and Roman Catholics and sought to offer a wider curriculum than that of the long-established universities. It was the first, in 1878, to admit women as equals. Its ramifications are to be found far and wide not only in Bloomsbury but in many parts of London. The College (left up Gower Street on a short detour) is classical in design, by William Wilkins, who was responsible for the much criticized National Gallery. The critics have been kinder to him about this building which has been subjected to many additions and alterations. It houses the Slade Art School, a gallery of painting by

Work and Play
Tottenham Street Mural
(opposite)

Senate House
University of London

ex-students of that establishment, and a collection of sculptures by John Flaxman.

Part of the inspiration behind University College came from the philosopher Jeremy Bentham who literally left his body to it. His auto-icon, as it is called, is preserved in a coffin which is on view during term-time.

Retrace your footsteps down Gower Street until you reach Torrington Place again. We are now truly in Bloomsbury and will remain in it for the rest of the walk apart from one brief foray into St Pancras and another into Gray's Inn. In architectural terms its dominant feature is of domesticity in fine squares and mostly more modest terraces; culturally, at personal level, it is inseparable from that group of writers and artists already mentioned and, at institutional level, it means the British Museum, the Courtauld and, of course, the University. Much of it is on land where stood the fortified manor of the de Belmund family but they came over with the Conqueror, or not long after, and trace of them has long since gone. Many street names are connected with the Russell family, and a large area of it is the Bedford Estate. The most famous member of the dynasty in this century was the philosopher Bertrand Russell but he was not a member of the Bloomsbury Group and did not, so far as I know, live here.

Occupying one whole side of Torrington Place is Dillon's University Bookshop in a fussy, non-purpose-built neo-Gothic block on four levels. Una Dillon had a small shop in Store Street, off Tottenham Court Road, when the university offered to back her in providing a fully-fledged campus bookshop which she ran successfully for many years.

Since her retirement the business has been sold by the university and is again in private hands. Its main entrance is in Malet Street facing the University Union building around which the students mill.

Next we make for Woburn Square, via Byng Place, the continuation of Torrington Place. Most of the buildings we pass have some connection with the university. Woburn Square has been quite ruined visually by the replacement of a nineteenth-century terrace with a hulking modern students' hostel. The reason for visiting it is the Courtauld Institute's gallery which has amongst other glories a sensational collection of French impressionists. It is at the end of a quite ordinary row of buildings and you ascend to the gallery in a capacious goods lift.

Samuel Courtauld was an industrialist and patron of the arts, who encouraged the Warburg Institute, an influential body in forming cultural taste, to come from Hamburg to be housed here, who bought pictures for the Tate out of his own funds and whose private collection is on view free of charge. The two rooms of his wonderful collection of impressionists and post-impressionists are thrilling. Here you can see a Monet of autumn at Argenteuil, a Cézanne of Mont Sainte Victoire, Manet's enigmatic *Bar aux Folies Bergères*, and a smaller version of his *Le Déjeuner sur l'herbe*. An earnest young French girl informed me, as we looked at the beautiful nude enjoying a picnic, that this picture is 'vairy sem-i-NAL'. There are also works by Degas, Gauguin, Renoir, Sisley, Toulouse-Lautrec and Camille Pissarro. This is the poor man's Jeu de Paume and, in one way, it has the edge on the great Paris collection because it is never so crowded. The present gallery is just the right size for the impressionists but too small to accommodate everything else it has accepted, so that not everything can be shown at the same time. The Fry Collection, including works by members of the Bloomsbury Group, is usually on view, but the Princes Gate Collection, bequeathed in 1978, has given the curator severe and unresolved problems. Not all the Lee, Witt and Gambier-Perry Collections may be viewed either and it is a pity so much has been accepted. The particular attraction of the present small gallery will be lost if the whole has to be removed elsewhere in order to be adequately displayed.

Gordon Square, standing immediately north of Woburn Square, has received kinder treatment than its smaller neighbour but still has to bear with traffic. London is a living city, not a museum, and the squares of Bloomsbury and elsewhere cannot be preserved in cloistered calm. That they still exist as imperfectly as they do after two centuries or so of development and war is a cause for rejoicing. That they all retain their central areas of green, even if some of them are for residents only, is a positive advantage environmentally.

On the east side of Gordon Square there are plaques to the biographer Lytton Strachey and the economist Maynard Keynes. Economics could be said to be more of a science than an art but Keynes's membership of the Bloomsbury Group was never in question, if only because there never was, officially, a group. History has imposed upon those remarkable men and women, whom we think of as 'Bloomsbury', a framework they did not consciously acquire for themselves. Also in Gordon Square at No. 52 is the Percival David Foundation of Chinese Art, a collection of ceramics from the ninth to the nineteenth centuries. It is open at varying times on weekdays, but not on Sundays or bank holidays.

In the adjacent Tavistock Square, to which we pass via Endsleigh Place, is the Jewish Museum, one of the few open on Sunday mornings, a point worth remembering. It is in one large first-floor room of Woburn House and is primarily concerned with items relating to Anglo-Jewry.

Tavistock Square has a most beautiful west side, preserved and/or restored in all its original glory. It was laid out by Thomas Cubitt for the Russells and the 540-foot-long terrace survives intact overlooking gardens which are open to the public. In them are a statue to Mahatma Gandhi, and a tree, planted on 6 August 1967 by the Mayor of Camden, in memory of those who died at Hiroshima. The east side is entirely modern and includes BMA (British Medical Association) House with inner courtyards of splendour which may be observed through the gates. On a wall is a plaque to say that Dickens lived in a house somewhere close by.

Walk northwards along Upper Woburn Place, with hotels on either side, until you come to Woburn Walk, a pretty paved way. Two three-storeyed terraces to Cubitt's original design, with bow-fronted shop windows, face each other and the northern one turns the corner into Duke's Road. You are soon at the rear of the parish church of St Pancras and able to note the replicas of the caryatids of the Erechtheum which have been added to each side, but they are not really supporting very much, and certainly not the lovely Inwood steeple popping up behind the temple pediment much like the one at St Martin's which so upsets the purists.

A good reason for stepping out on to the pavement of noisy Euston Road is to look down (or even go down) to the St Pancras Hotel and railway station. This is by Sir George Gilbert Scott whose Albert Memorial we have already inspected. Why do I like one and not the other? Because the hotel and station are neither pompous nor pretentious and because the design is quite unexpected. Presumably to allow for a drive-in forecourt, the mass of the building lies back from the road at a slight angle but that didn't inhibit Scott from giving one end a curved wing of twelve bays which takes over the pavement with a short colonnade. The forecourt itself is imaginatively dealt with in a ramp rising to an archway leading into the station. Up to five storeys the hotel is a conventional and solid item of Victorian Gothic but above Scott let rip with a riot of turrets, chimney-stacks, dormer windows, crenellations, balconies and, at the non-winged end, a clock tower with lantern, spire and weathervane. Scholars may pinpoint this detail and that as heavily derivative but Scott, who was steeped in medievalism, brought them together with a unique stamp and the roofscape is sheer ecstasy. This masterpiece has not functioned as a hotel for many decades and is now used as offices by British Rail. Behind it lies W. H. Barlow's expansive train shed of 1868. It is 690 feet long and has a span of 243 feet.

We must return, however, past those tireless caryatids to Duke's Road and across to Burton Place which leads into Cartwright Gardens. Here you join the two exquisite terraces at a break in the crescent. The elegant, balconied residences are now mostly small private hotels which look out upon tennis courts and flowerbeds, and on to the Commonwealth Hall of the University of London which is partly hidden by trees (which is no loss).

Bear right into Marchmont Street at the end of which is the Brunswick Centre looking like a barracks capable of being transformed into a fortress if required. It was intended to be the answer to high-rise inner-city residential blocks and, at least, it does not go up to skyscraper level. The successive storeys lie back ramp-like above each other on two enormous bases running north–south, and are joined by catwalks over a central avenue round which shops and a cinema are grouped. The flats have balconies, some glassed-in, others open, and fire escapes ending in mid air lie against windows. Trailing foliage can be observed but in the avenue where there should be grass there are flagstones and a few flowerbeds. Unfortunately it is all in

Euston Road
Reflection of
Post Office Tower

concrete which makes it drab, drab, drab. It was completed in the early 1970s and it has altered the geography of this part of Bloomsbury. Somewhere under its greyness lies the site of No. 40 Coram Street where once I had 'a little back room' in a typical Bedford Estate terrace house. It is numbing not to be able to identify where I lived, makes me feel it was perhaps a dream and that the people who shared the house with me were fictional. Perhaps William Makepeace Thackeray, who lived in the same street where the Bloomsbury Hotel now spreads itself, would feel the same if he could see what has been done to Coram Street and Brunswick Square. The latter retains its shape and it must be understood that it never had houses on its eastern side, nor did Mecklenburgh Square on its western. Once the Foundling Hospital, on Coram's Fields, stood between them. Now it is open space. Thomas Coram, a sea captain who cared for illegitimate and orphaned children, is remembered by a museum at 40 Brunswick Square where the work of the Foundation named after him goes on and where there is a rather uninteresting collection of pictures, although a jolly portrait of the captain himself by Hogarth enhances the first-floor landing. The Fields are now the Harmsworth Memorial Playground, the gate into which you are adjured to keep shut to protect the kids. There is a notice: 'No admission for unaccompanied adults.'

Leave Brunswick Square by Lansdowne Terrace and go left into Guilford Street. After the entrance to the Fields go left again into Mecklenburgh Place, leading into the square. There is a plaque to R. H. Tawney, the political philosopher, but not to the Woolfs who moved here, with their Hogarth Press, after being bombed out of Tavistock Square. Leave the square by Doughty Street which crosses Guilford Street. Along on the left is No. 48 where Charles Dickens lived from 1837 to 1839. It is now a museum on four floors crammed with mementoes of the novelist's life, with a large library of books by and about him. The house was saved from destruction in 1922 by the Dickens Trust. You ring for admission and are welcomed in formally in the ground-floor front room where a short lecture is delivered before you are permitted to tour the house alone. In the basement is the library and pleasant 'ye olde tea roome' table and chairs. You may not enter the stillroom where a table is set for a simple meal, nor the wash-house which looks most primitive. In the passage is a model of the Maypole Inn featured in *Barnaby Rudge*. On the ground floor you can see a desk at which Dickens worked and one wall bears a large family tree. In the bedroom, on the second floor, is the Frith portrait and also a photograph of an early study for it. The contrast is interesting. In the study Dickens looks harassed; in the final portrait he is erect, perfectly composed. In another bedroom is a backcloth painted by Clarkson Stanfield, the marine painter, for Wilkie Collins's play *The Lighthouse* in which Dickens and the author acted. So did the artist Augustus Egg and a Mr Crummles. The performance took place at 'the Smallest Theatre in the World' in Tavistock House, in 1855. This was an earlier Bloomsbury Group; a comparative study of the two will surely be written. (The house is open on weekdays, 10–5; there is a small admission charge.)

Doughty Street becomes John Street and you leave it, turning right into Theobald's Road, opposite Gray's Inn. Here, as in Lincoln's Inn and the Temple, barristers have their chambers, solicitors their offices and aspiring members of the legal profession study. Gray's Inn dates back to the fourteenth century, or earlier, and has had many, many distinguished residents. Francis Bacon wrote his essays here and in the

Hall the first performance of Shakespeare's *A Comedy of Errors* was given. This seems appropriate although, alas, the errors of the law are sometimes tragic. Lawyers have a knack of building themselves into serene surroundings and Gray's Inn is no exception, although that did not allow it to escape from the bombing which destroyed its hall and chapel.

Turn left out of Theobald's Road into Bedford Row, a wide tree-lined Georgian street where there has been successful restoration. Half-way down on the right is Princeton Street which leads across Red Lion Street (formerly Lamb's Conduit Street) into what is left of Red Lion Square. The west side has been swept completely away along with Little Red Lion Street, to make a wide road between Theobald's and High Holborn. The central garden has been kept and in it is a bust to Bertrand Russell who would certainly have been familiar with the Conway Hall, home of the South Place Ethical Society and a meeting-place for dissenters in general. It stands on the north-east side of the square, along from the reclining statue of Pocahontas, here called *La Belle Sauvage*. On the south side a pleasant terrace survives.

Take your life in your hands as you cross the great gap to the pavement outside the Polytechnic of London's School of Law which has an attractive item of stained glass in its entrance hall.

There is a slightly easier way of reconnecting yourself with Theobald's Road which bypasses the Law School and this you could well judge to be the sensible way to get across the traffic. It involves two zebras, and it is quite absurd to have to mention it, but there is no easy way for a pedestrian to get from Red Lion Square to the Central School, standing on a corner of Theobald's Road and Southampton Row. The solid and quite unremarkable-looking building which we are not even going to look into has significance because of its association with the Arts and Crafts Movement.

The movement was inspired by William Morris, Victorian artist craftsman and writer himself, who was alarmed because he feared that increasing industrialization would lead to debased standards of workmanship. More realistically, W. R. Lethaby, who became the first Principal of the Central School of Arts and Crafts, created by the then newly founded London County Council in 1896, saw that science had come to stay and that artists and craftsmen should benefit from its discoveries, using it to further their own inspiration. In the past quarter of a century the school has expanded both conceptually and physically. It has annexes for sculpture, weaving, knitting and ceramics, and is connected with the adjoining Jeannetta Cochrane Theatre. In 1967 its name was changed to the Central School of Art and Design. It sponsors, in addition to full-time degree courses, evening classes in the subjects for which it caters. It is part of that splendid system of adult education which gives everyone a second chance to study after they have escaped from the hang-ups of the classroom. All this may be far from your mind as you concentrate, once again, on the traffic problem and getting across Southampton Row which is here divided by what was the entrance to the tramway tunnel to the Embankment. The last tram ground its way down here on 6 April 1952, and part of the tunnel has been converted into a useful road running from Waterloo Bridge under Aldwych and out into Kingsway. Why it wasn't extended this far I don't know. On your way into Bloomsbury Square dally a few minutes in Sicilian Avenue which runs obliquely between Southampton Row and Bloomsbury Way. It consists of smallish shops on either side of a marble pavement. Above them are offices (once they were flats) with turrets and stone balconies. At each end are purely decorative, pillared entrances which do nothing to support the buildings, nor are they supported by them. They are just a little Sicilian and date from 1905.

Bloomsbury Square is marred by the enormity of the Liverpool Insurance building which occupies the entire east side and fronts on to Southampton Row. It looks as though the architect had planned to imitate the Parthenon, and then, noting a declining interest in religion, changed his mind and settled for offices. Its presence affects the balance of the square most miserably whereas the car-park dug out beneath it has left the garden intact with all its trees and flowers, and a statue of Charles James Fox, eighteenth-century statesman, togged up as a Roman senator. On the north side are houses with pretty ironwork balconies.

Proceed along Bloomsbury Way to see St George's, the parish church of Bloomsbury, designed by Nicholas Hawksmoor. It gives the impression of being determined to repulse all attempts to oust it. There is scarcely any churchyard. Streets and office-cum-apartment blocks hem it in. It is dirty but not altogether unloved. The classical frontage seems to me much too tall and heavy for the available space but I like the way the tower is set to one side yet is still an integral part of the whole, not a separate campanile. Hawksmoor let himself go with the tower which spirals up to a statue of George I way above an imitation of the mausoleum at Halicarnassus. The inside is light and tranquil and in it organ recitals are given on some weekdays.

Turn right into Museum Street (several bookshops, some pub-lishers' offices and a good tavern) which leads to Great Russell Street and the British Museum. This is a noble building, having a noble purpose. It houses priceless treasures behind its massive neo-classical frontage with a busily-sculpted pediment and portico above triple lines of pillars. It is reached across a forecourt sufficiently grand for what it heralds and the car-parking thereon is moderately discreet.

On a single visit you will sample only a fraction of what the BM has on show. Its curator has the inevitable problem of wishing to preside over a growing collection but having insufficient space for new exhibits. The museum was founded in 1753 on the private collection of Sir Hans Sloane (see Walk Three) and it nearly came to be accommodated in Buckingham House. This, however, was thought to be too expensive a home so Montague House, in Bloomsbury, was taken instead and there, mainly over the next century and a half, the present museum was built. Parts of the collection have been hived off to other centres, noted elsewhere in this book, and the National Library will be moved to a site now being prepared for it near St Pancras station.

*The bespoke
Umbrella Shop
New Oxford Street
(to be seen from
Museum Street)*

Railings
British Museum

The bulk of the collection remains here, and will do so, apart possibly from the Parthenon friezes, known as the Elgin Marbles. There is a move to have them returned to Athens where they originated, but it should be stated firmly that Lord Elgin did not steal them. He brought them here with permission from their owners and they are preserved thanks to him and to those to whom they were entrusted. They are superbly displayed in the gallery, and should they ever return to Athens I hope they will be as beautifully displayed there. Surely they will be because current Athenian museum standards are of the highest.

There is no space here to even begin to discuss the other stunning exhibits in the BM. Equip yourself with one of the plans freely available in the entrance hall and, as the mood takes you, make for the Greek and Roman, the Oriental or the Egyptian departments. Allow yourself to be attracted by coins and medals, prints and drawings, illuminated manuscripts or early maps. There are chambers full of early clocks – one in the shape of a golden galleon – and watches and you may examine them in rather gloomy lighting against a background of chiming. There are carved twelfth-century chessmen from Scandinavia; a statue of Apollo armless, yet playing his lyre; the Nereid Room with a temple reconstruction at the end of it softly lit against pale blue walls. There is the wonderful head of King Rameses II of Egypt looking benignly down on the surrounding sculptures of human and mythical beings. Many early books are on display, including the first printed by Caxton at Westminster, and a Gutenberg Bible. There is Shaw's *Saint Joan* manuscript in short-hand, and an 1899 edition of *The Importance of Being Earnest*, one of twelve copies printed on Japanese vellum. There are totem poles and Buddhas and wondrous Greek vases. There is almost too much. I have mentioned, as always in this book, only some of my favourites.

In addition to what is permanently displayed, special exhibitions are regularly mounted and sometimes draw embarrassingly huge crowds.

The BM is open all weekdays from 10 to 5 and on Sundays 2.30 to 6. It is closed, alas, on most public holidays. Admission is free. There are regular lectures and films, licensed refreshments and wheelchair facilities for the disabled.

When you leave by the northern exit from the Edward VII Gallery you are in Montague Place. Along to the left is Bedford Square, the best-preserved of the squares on the Bedford Estate, even though three lanes of traffic pass down its east side in an almost continual stream throughout the day; on the right is Russell Square where you can relax. The gardens in Bedford Square are private but it is worth a visit because the terraces on all four sides are almost complete, even though parts of some of them have been heavily restored. A few errors have crept in – attic windows owing nothing to an earlier century and spacious rooms rudely partitioned to meet office requirements – but the exteriors are mostly maintained in the spirit of their original design. Camden Council has narrowed the roadway on three sides and established what is almost a piazza, and you may no longer park, even on a meter.

Russell Square, where this walk ends, is dominated by the Senate House of London University, a simple, dignified structure, more acceptable than much of what it overlooks. For nearly fifty years an area beneath it was not built upon – war and planning blight afflicted it – but work is now proceeding and what has been erected so far is neutrally neo-Georgian. There is little of architectural glory surrounding the gardens of the square which is curiously unlittered by sculptures and statuary. There is only Francis, fifth Duke of Bedford, in agricultural attire staring down Bedford Place at the aforementioned Roman Fox in Bloomsbury Square. A more humble monument

Portico
British Museum
(opposite)

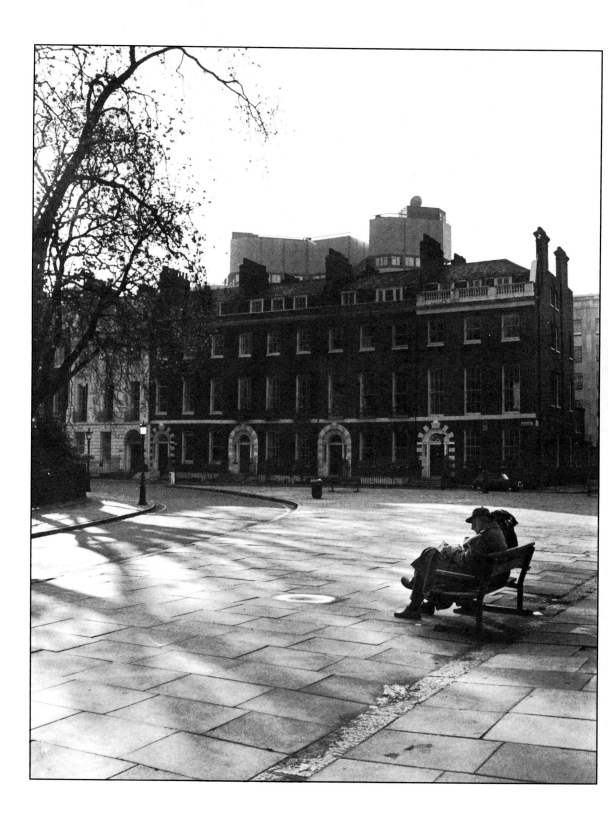

is a tree planted by Lady Barbirolli, in 1973, in memory of her conductor husband, Sir John. Alas, it doesn't seem to be doing well.

So there is little to see and that is as well after our long walk. Whenever I am here I see triffids. John Wyndham, who disliked his work being classified as Science Fiction, lived near by when he wrote his masterpiece. So did I, when I read it. His murderous plants found victims here in Russell Square but you should be safe from them as you lie on the grass or take refreshment at the café, which is open all the year round.

Sunday morning
Bedford Square
(opposite)

Walk Seven

Trafalgar Square – National Gallery – Pall Mall –
St James's – Piccadilly – Burlington Arcade –
Berkeley Square – Bond Street – Manchester Square –
Grosvenor Square – Shepherd Market – Apsley House –
Hyde Park – Speakers' Corner – Marble Arch

Royal Arcade
Bond Street
(opposite)

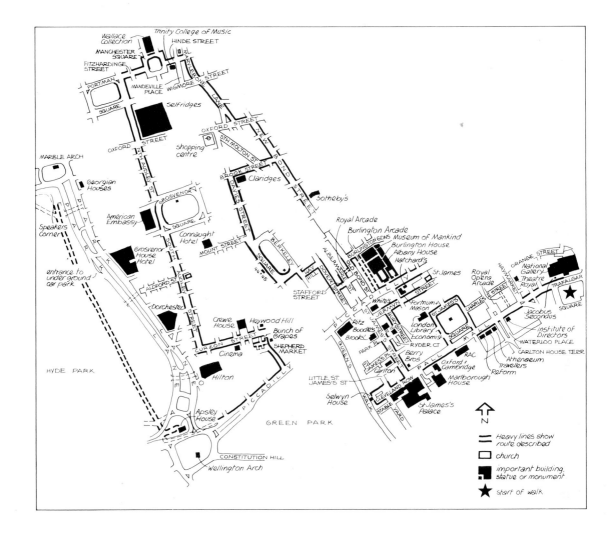

Before leaving Nelson's square on this occasion we at last go into the National Gallery. Far less than half of the building you enter under the central portico is by Wilkins, whose brief was simply to design, on a long narrow site, a suitable depository for a small collection of paintings formerly belonging to John Julius Angerstein.

Britain was later than most leading European countries in establishing a national collection, and might have been later still had not the Austrian government repaid two loans advanced to them in the 1790s to secure their alliance in fighting the French. The Treasury paid £57,000 to Angerstein for thirty-eight paintings and the National Gallery was, somewhat ignominiously, born. Since then the building has been extended many times to form what was, until the mid 1970s, a rectangle with several inner courtyards. The last extension was added to the north-west end in 1973–75 and includes a separate entrance from Orange Street.

The collection which began so modestly has remained so, when compared with others in Vienna, Florence, Madrid, Paris, but this, so the present director, Sir Michael Levey, believes, has made possible the most 'sheerly balanced and representative of all national collections of European paintings'. That is a matter for scholars. What is beyond doubt is the excellence of so many of the pictures, which attract two million visitors each year. Use Homan Potterton's Guide to find your way around. It is cross-referenced, with one index for artists and another for room numbers. It has illustrations, in black and white, of over one hundred and fifty paintings, and is based on the more detailed guides in which the entire collection is illustrated with commentaries.

The National Gallery is open, free, every day but not on Sunday mornings. There are paintings for every mood if you will allow them to work their magic. Maybe Degas's *La La at the Cirque Fernando*, hanging by her teeth from a trapeze, will attract you, or Velasquez's *Rokeby Venus* admiring herself in a mirror, or Van Dyck's *Charles I on Horseback*. There surely must be something here to which you will respond. I shall adapt the long-running radio programme, and play Desert Island Daubs, listing the eight canvases I would take with me if I were marooned on a mid-ocean shore. Choice No. 1 is El Greco's *Christ driving the Traders from the Temple* because it was the first painting I ever really looked at, returning again and again from other rooms in the gallery to be held spellbound by its composition and bold colours. There is so much action and reaction in it, such strength. When I bought a rather poor reproduction to hang on my bedroom wall my mother worried that I had 'got' religion.

National Gallery
(opposite)

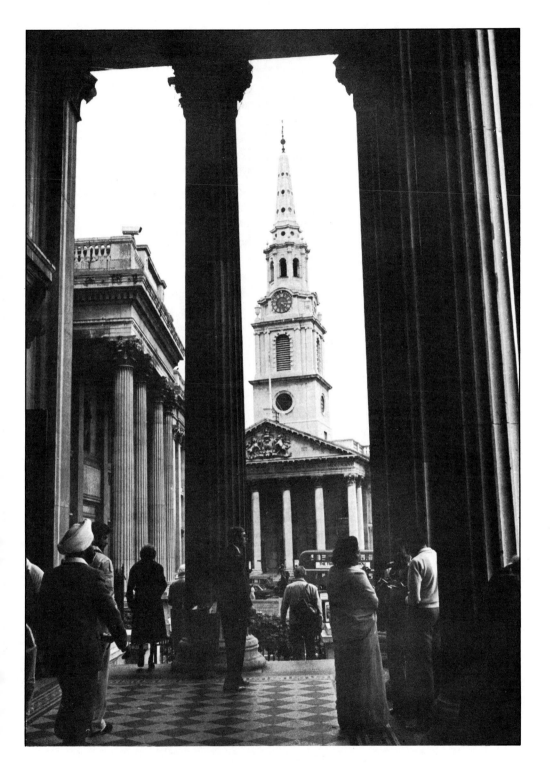

Because it belongs to the same period of my life I would have to take Jan van Eyck's 'The Arnolfini marriage' which I read about in Thomas Bodkin's *Approach to Painting* before I went to look at it. How practical of that prissy, unsmiling man in the outsize hat to conduct his own marriage ceremony (as he was entitled to) with the lady whom he had already made pregnant.

Next comes Turner's *The Fighting Téméraire* because it represents the first occasion I can recall when I went on sudden impulse to a gallery to look at one particular work. The sailing warship is being towed on its last journey to the breaker's yard by a steam tug. The fantastic golden sunset is both real and symbolic. Fourth has to be a Rembrandt portrait, but which? The elderly Margaretha Trip, in her snow-white ruff, the *Old Man in an Armchair,* the *Woman Bathing in a Stream*, or a *Self-Portrait?* Each has the same probing quality, capturing a unique moment. I will have to draw lots.

Fifth shall be Caravaggio's *The Supper at Emmaus*. I don't know if Rembrandt was influenced by him, though it is probable he was aware of his work, but in Caravaggio there is a similar drama of light and shade as with the subtler Dutch master. Caravaggio goes in for the big effect. Look at the splayed-out thumb and fingers of the man on the left of Christ.

Hobbema comes next, quite irrationally, with his *Avenue at Middelharnis*. Although it is a landscape with skinny trees in Holland it makes me think of driving down great green avenues towards the Mediterranean. Whilst in Holland I must include Pieter de Hoogh's *The Courtyard of a House in Delft* because I would be able to gaze at it for hours, always finding something new in the relationship between the mother in the right-hand section and the woman with her back to the artist down the corridor on the left.

Eighth and last has to be an impressionist, although most of my favourites are in the Jeu de Paume or the Courtauld. I will settle for Renoir's *Les Parapluies*.

This leaves a great many pictures still hanging on the walls, so it is reasonable, lest the ones I have selected are being restored or on loan to other galleries at the time of my shipwreck, to choose eight substitutes. They shall be whichever three Rembrandt portraits lost in the lottery, Piero della Francesca's Nativity, a subject for which I have a rather low tolerance level when I am trundling around Italian galleries, but this one is different. The Christ child is lying on the floor on his back and giving as much adulation to the kneeling mother as she is according him, and I love those pallid-faced musicians pretending to play their stringless lutes.

A Botticelli tondo, *The Adoration of the Kings*, shall be fifth because of all those bustling Florentines, some of whom are ogling the camera. It would be a reminder of happy holidays spent in Italy, as would Canaletto's *Basin of San Marco on Ascension Day*. This leaves room for two more, so it is back to France for Corot's *Avignon from the West* with its incomparable view of the Provencal landscape and Monet's *The Water-Lily Pond* painted at Giverny, with the Chinese bridge over which I have walked (or think I have, and I don't wish to know if it's a reconstruction).

If you have spent the morning in the National Gallery remain in it for lunch. In the basement is an excellent cafeteria with hot and cold dishes at, for London, reasonable prices. Only the house wine is sub-standard but even that deserves to be served in something better than thick tumblers.

When you leave turn right past the statue of 'Jacobus Secondus', as is described the second James who was King for a mercifully short period at the end of the seventeenth century. Beyond the end of Wilkins's frontage is the site for the next gallery extension which, I pray, will not be a monument to hi-tech. There has, as always, been controversy about the designs submitted and one leading architect has made it clear that he would welcome something resembling the Centre Pompidou.

Walk along to Pall Mall and enter clubland. Englishmen adore clubs and their exclusiveness and the whole heady business of having their names 'put in the book', and of being, in due course, elected, unless they are blackballed. In the twenty years after the Second World War many of the clubs had a thin time, some closed down, others amalgamated, but the survivors now seem to be thriving again and there is no shortage of those willing to pay a three-figure entrance fee and a higher annual subscription. One which did not last occupied the present Institute of Directors on the corner of Waterloo Place. Nash designed it for the United Services Club, whose members relaxed on horsehair settees and armchairs in vast drawing-rooms, and were served indifferently cooked meals. When I was a guest there it was always crowded so I don't know why it failed. As the Institute of Directors it probably still serves some of its old members. The building faces the Athenaeum across the Place and both have friezes below their cornices, the Athenaeum's in dark blue, the Directors' in light, but so far as I know there is no relation between this and the Oxbridge rowing colours. Decimus Burton, who remodelled Nash's building, designed the Athenaeum, and a very noble pile it is with a grand staircase rising at the back of the deep vestibule and dividing to reach the library, where I have observed actual bishops in actual gaiters.

Waterloo Place

Next to the Athenaeum is the Travellers'. It was here that Phileas Fogg arrived in the nick of time to discover that he *had* been around the world in eighty days. Or was it at the Reform, which is next door? The latter, I think. Both are architectural emblems of the enduring qualities of Victorian England, both are by Charles Barry. The Reform has a spacious marbled entrance-hall which, with its colonnades, is more like a piazza. It becomes a bar at lunchtime and this gives it a faintly illicit air. You feel as though you were tippling in church. After lunch in the long elegant dining-room looking out upon Carlton House Terrace, you ascend to a balcony overlooking the 'piazza' to take coffee or port. The Reform now admits women to membership. In view of its name it could hardly do otherwise, and it is only surprising that a Pankhurst didn't force her way in earlier in the century.

Before going further down Pall Mall which is, incidentally, the name of an old ball game, played with a hammer, perhaps popular here, we should go into St James's Square. One entrance off the north side will take us in, another out. There are gardens in the centre of the square, administered by the St James's Square Trust, and open Monday to Friday, 10–4.30. You may sit on the grass and give yourself a restful lesson in architecture as your eye roves round the buildings of many different periods. There is nothing too monstrous to behold and if you look due east down Charles II Street there is a splendid view of the Theatre Royal in the Haymarket which we come to in the next walk. Very little dates back to the late seventeenth century when the square was laid out: there is more from the eighteenth, and still more from the nineteenth. There is a statue to William III, who is classically dressed and on horseback, and the molehill which caused his death when his mount stumbled on it and threw him, is there also. In the north-west corner of the square is the London Library, one of the few surviving private subscription libraries, much depended upon by authors doing research.

Back to Pall Mall which you cross opposite the RAC Club. It is the largest but least prestigious of them all. Go west, past plaques to Thomas Gainsborough and Nell Gwynne, the Oxford and Cambridge Club which is unisex, to Marlborough House which was built by Christopher Wren for the Duke and Duchess of that ilk. After the death of George V it became the home of his widow, Queen Mary, and is now used for official receptions and conferences. When it is not in use it is open at weekends and on bank holidays, ground floor only. Conducted tours include the very fine saloon with windows on to a spacious garden.

St James's Palace, which was also a royal residence longer ago, is at the end of Pall Mall. It is a homely-looking palace, despite the sentry on the door, built in dark brick for Henry VIII on the site of a leper hospital. Not a lot of his palace remains though the state apartments, redesigned by Wren, are said to be very fine. But it is rarely possible to see them and you must rely on the descriptions given in Pevsner and elsewhere, which is tantalizing. At least you can enjoy, near where the sentry stands, the overhanging bay which adds very much to the domestic qualities of the building. Although it is nearly two centuries since this was a royal residence ambassadors are still accredited to the Court of St James.

The surrounding streets are worth inspecting. A narrower extension to Pall Mall is Cleveland Row off which runs Stable Yard. Facing, as you pass the palace, is a fine five-storey building with an iron balcony at first-floor level. It is now used as offices, so neon lighting has been installed and this spoils it a little. Next, across an even narrower opening, but still in Cleveland Row, is Selwyn House which is delightful from the front, but walk to the rear where you can see a three-bayed and balconied first floor facing a roof garden above the heavily rusticated and entranceless ground floor. It overlooks Green Park as do all the houses with gardens bordering the Queen's Walk which stretches up to Piccadilly: a most privileged position.

Return along Cleveland Row to St James's Street and cross it to admire a group of shops which includes Berry Bros. & Rudd, wine

merchants; Lock's, hatters; and Lobb's, shoemakers. Berry Brothers have had these premises for over 250 years, although they now have a country warehouse where most of their stock is accommodated. You enter by a seventeenth-century door on to creaking, sloping floorboards, and are courteously but not obsequiously greeted. The original address was 'at the sign of the coffee mill', coffee being one of the commodities supplied to the Court of St James and to the noblemen who hung about it. Nowadays, and for ninety years or more, Berry Bros. has dealt only in wines and spirits. I have no firsthand experience of the other two retailers because I don't wear hats or go in for handmade shoes, but I expect that those who do get the same exquisite service as at the wine merchants.

Quite out of keeping with all this old-world graciousness, on the corner of Little St James's Street, is a fierce-looking bronze-coloured construction which resembles a space rocket trapped into its surroundings. In St James's Place at No. 4, Chopin stayed in 1848 and from here he went to the Guildhall to give his last public recital. (Another plaque to him is at 99 Eaton Place where he also performed in the same last tragic year of his life.)

In St James's Street there are also clubs but of a more exclusive nature than those in Pall Mall, and occupying more modest premises. Boodle's is one of them, with a pillared and pedimented first-floor window and, at ground level, a very handsome bow. It is said to have an Adam saloon with a finely-worked ceiling but Pevsner says it is only 'Adamish'. It began life as a betting club. A few doors away is White's which David Piper describes as 'the most arrogant of all London clubs', and there are also the Carlton and Brooks's, the latter on the corner of Park Place in a style which again suggests Adam but is actually by Henry Holland. I feel that The Drones should be somewhere close at hand, and Wodehousians may well believe it is, but I haven't actually located it. Of those which can be seen by the passer-by, Boodle's is the most interesting as well as pleasing club. You can peer in at members in the ground floor fastness and they can (indeed, do) peer back at you haughtily, maintaining an implacable defence against the real world.

Opposite Brooks's are steps, and a ramp, into Ryder Court, the *Economist* newspaper's complex of three buildings of varying height (four, eight and fifteen storeys) in Portland stone. They are faceless but unobjectionable, and Henry Moore's large *Reclining Connected Forms*, placed between two of them, seems an appropriate decoration. Leave by steps into Bury Street, turn left, then right, into Jermyn Street, famous for its gentlemen's outfitters, in one of which you can buy any club tie that takes your fancy if you have the nerve to ask for

Lock's the Hatters
St James's Street
(opposite)

Boodles, St James's Street
backed by
Economist *complex*

it. Opposite Russell and Bromley are steps up into the garden of St James's, Piccadilly, one entrance to which is next to the Wren Coffee Rooms. But the church is best approached by the passage at its east end, which bring you out into Piccadilly by a brass-rubbing centre with a signboard urging you to 'Take Home a Knight from Mediaeval England'.

St James's is a Wren church lying along Piccadilly across a sloping entrance-yard. Its lovely light interior was restored after being bombed in the Second World War. The work of Grinling Gibbons escaped, having been removed to safety. His font, organ and reredos were returned when the church was rededicated in 1954. There is a gallery round three sides with decoration in gold and white. The main entrance was originally from Jermyn Street because the church was built to serve the new estate laid out around St James's Square by Henry Jermyn, Earl of St Alban's. It has become the parish church of the Royal Academy who are across Piccadilly in Burlington House. A piccadill is a decorative border on a collar and those who once made them worked around here, so that could be the origin of the street name. It is one of London's best-known thoroughfares, celebrated in many songs, and at its eastern end is the famous circus. We come to it on our next walk; on this occasion we turn westwards. On the south side is Hatchard's, with double-bow windows, established in 1797 and considered to be London's most prestigious bookshop, and Fortnum and Mason, a very superior emporium where top people shop for takeaway caviare. If you are not in a mood to buy either books or edible delicacies cross Piccadilly and walk along the north side past the Piccadilly Hotel (by Norman Shaw), Albany and Burlington House. Albany – the definite article is not used – is a late-eighteenth-century house, approached across a forecourt, which was converted into apartments around 1800. Once it was only for bachelors. Now ladies are permitted to reside here also, but not children. It has many associations with authors and artists and many who rent apartments here use them as second homes, convenient London *pieds-à-terre*. It is private property but no one will object if you walk into the forecourt and look. Behind the frontage are covered passages and iron staircases leading to open corridors, which makes it look like a prison. Amongst those who lived here were Byron, Macaulay, Bulwer Lytton, Compton Mackenzie, Harold Nicolson, Kenneth Clark.

Burlington House, the home of the Royal Academy, is further to the west. The Academy confers status upon painters when it accepts their work for the annual exhibition. To be hung, even below the line, is an honour: to be elected a Royal Academician (the numbers are limited to forty at any one time) is the ultimate reward, though not all artists feel this. The first exhibition was held in 1769 in Somerset House, after George III had been persuaded to establish an academy. Sir Joshua Reynolds was the first president (his statue is in the courtyard) but not all of our greatest artists have followed in his wake because the RA has a long history of resistance to new movements in art. There is a permanent collection housed on the top floor consisting of works deposited with the Academy by its members and therefore including paintings by Turner, Constable, Gainsborough, etc., but these are exhibited only occasionally, as is another treasure, the only marble statue in Britain by Michelangelo, his unfinished *Madonna Taddei*. Formerly the Academy owned a Leonardo cartoon but this was sold to the National Gallery for £800,000 to stave off bankruptcy. Apart from the summer exhibition, at which the paintings are for sale, there are regular exhibitions, many of which attract large crowds which line the courtyard and the pavement in Piccadilly, waiting for admission. Burlington House lies back from the street behind an arched gateway, and flanked by other buildings used by half a dozen learned societies. It has suffered much conversion since it was erected in 1664 and many of our best-known architects have had a hand in its evolution. (For £15 you can become a friend and attend openings.)

Turn right when you leave the courtyard and walk along to the entrance to the Burlington Arcade. Before entering look further down Piccadilly on the other side to note the Ritz Hotel. César Ritz, a Swiss hotelier, gave his name to the language, and to this Edwardian hotel in the French style with a colonnade over the street in front of it. When my daughter saw through the pretensions of the Charing Cross Hotel she demanded a birthday tea here. She was disappointed; the Ritz has nothing to compete with British Rail's marble but its name has greater cachet. I tried to end a walk with tea here but it has not worked out that way.

Turn your attention to the Arcade where you may observe a uniformed man in a top hat and morning coat. He is a beadle and employed to patrol this covered way, not much wider than a saloon car, which runs through to Burlington Gardens, where there is not a flowerbed or a patch of grass in sight. Burlington is quite the most handsome of the arcades visited on this walk and the next, and is lined, on both sides, with small shops selling jewellery, cutlery, clothes, china, and any sort of merchandise thought to be attractive to tourists with great stashes of credit cards in their wallets. At Burlington Bertie's you can buy, from a miscellaneous assortment of souvenirs, articles you might well not find anywhere else. (It is an unsuitable name because the Bert of the music-hall song was a down-and-out who mocked at social pretensions – 'I'm Bert, Bert, I haven't a shirt, but my people are well off you know', etc.) Other shops are called Noble Jones, Lord Shirtmaker, Berk, and Yeo, the latter two short names reminiscent of ancient streams, but none I think ran down here. The arcade was constructed in 1819. In 1969 Princess Alexandra unveiled a plaque to celebrate its sesquicentenary. In it, by one of those legal quirks of which we have heard more on our city walks, there is no right of way whatsoever, not even for American

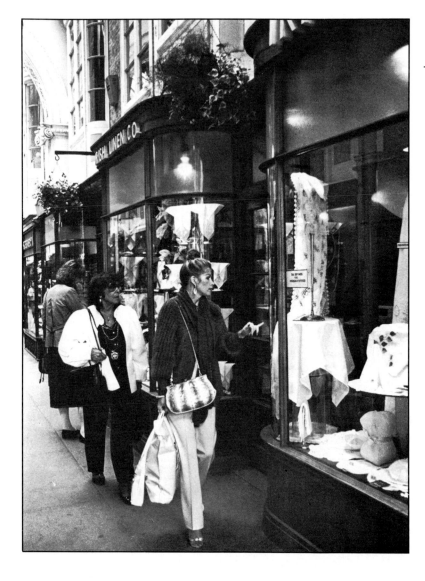

Burlington Arcade

Express cardholders, although I dare say the shopkeepers, and even the beadles, constantly overlook this. One Saturday morning, in the early 1970s, a large saloon car did drive into this sanctuary and, having robbed a jeweller's, reversed down most of its length at high speed to a successful getaway. Your exit will be more decorous. First turn right to visit the Museum of Mankind, a Victorian building which backs on to Burlington House. It is now the Ethnographic Department of the British Museum where temporary exhibitions are mounted to run in most instances concurrently for about a year. One may show how primitive tribes lived in Peru, another may do the same for a Bengal village. The flies and the stench will be absent but you can't have everything, and what is shown is invariably most imaginatively mounted.

Return past the entrance to the Arcade and on to New Bond Street where you turn left and it instantly becomes *Old* Bond Street. Just down on the right is the Royal Arcade, taller but much shorter than the Burlington, and more ostentatiously decorated at roof level. At the end go left into Albemarle Street, right into Stafford Street and right again into Dover Street, almost opposite Ely House. This was built for himself in the Palladian style by a Bishop who apparently had a splendid indifference to squeezing through the eye of a needle. It later became a club, and later still the offices of the Oxford University Press where I attended parties in its marbled halls. This cannot be counted upon for all readers, so proceed past Brown's Hotel, much favoured by American visitors for its genteel Englishness (Piper observes that not only is it the perfect place in which to read a Henry James novel, but to *be* in one) to Hay Hill, into which you turn left.

Cartier's
New Bond Street
(short detour required)

At the bottom of Hay Hill turn right and you are almost in Berkeley Square where the famous nightingale sang. Do not expect to hear it. More probably you will catch the siren songs of the classy car salesmen on the east side, or of the croupiers on the west. You are now in Mayfair which, until the early eighteenth century, was green fields, even hunting territory. At least it was developed with some reference to its previous appearance. There are no hedgerows now between the meadows, but there are many squares with grass and trees. Londoners, by which I mean the commuting workers as well as the residents, are grateful for this. How drear it would be if there were no interruptions to the streets and streets of houses, shops and offices.

Berkeley Square can look like a dusty waste in a long, dry summer but we don't have many of those. The only statue is of a nude nymph presented by the Marquess of Lansdowne in 1858. He lived in a house to the south of the square, which is now a club. Possibly the most eminent resident was Robert Clive (Clive of India), governor of Bengal, who lived and died at No. 45. He shot himself after being censured for his conduct in the sub-continent, and there is a plaque to him. Next door, at No. 44, William Kent designed the house which Service says 'is one of the supreme works of architecture in London'. You must join the gambling club which now occupies it to give a verdict on his opinion. Certainly the illustrations of the staircase and screen which he gives on page 62 of his book are stunning. Pevsner says it 'might well be called the finest terrace house in London' and also goes overboard about the interior. Shall the songs of the croupiers go unheard by us?

Leave Berkeley Square going north, but glance to your left along Mount Street, where amongst all the antique shops is a master butcher and also John Baily & Son (Poulters), est. 1720. Perhaps they supply the Connaught opposite, a grand hotel where your identity will be protected from prying journalists, where you can be as alone as a Garbo. But we are going towards another, even more famous, hotel, Claridge's, with its side entrance in Davies Street, and its front (turn right) in Brook Street. It is especially popular with visiting royalty who haven't been offered a kip at the palace, possibly because they have contrived to lose their thrones. When I was young and very impecunious it amused me to enter by Davies Street (door opened by uniformed flunkey), proceed to the central lobby where I looked about me importantly as though expecting several ex-crowned heads to rush forward in greeting, and then, on receiving absolutely no recognition at all, apart from a bellboy's jeering look, to leave by the Brook Street entrance (door opened by uniformed flunkey). I doubted that, in these security-conscious days, this would still be possible but my still impecunious publisher still makes a habit of it.

If your ego is less finely pointed than ours, just walk past Claridge's admiring its discreet exterior, and go towards New Bond Street again, passing the pedestrianized but otherwise rather uninteresting South Moulton Street, on your left. I confess I also find Bond Street, Old and New, yawnworthy. I love to buy it on the Monopoly board but its reality holds no allure for me, perhaps because I am not attracted to gold rings and salerooms. If you are you should linger here after turning right and go to a sale at Sotheby's. If not, retrace your steps with me to Oxford Street, another unfavourite London street of mine. Towards the left is Bond Street tube station with a particularly hideous modern shopping centre over and beside it, all blaring and glaring. *Cross* Oxford Street, which is what I always tend to do, rather than mill along it with the crowds who spread out into its many department stores, and make for Marylebone Lane which comes before the tube station. Try to imagine what it was like when it was a lane in Mayfair, much the shape it is now but without the buildings. Cross Wigmore Street (in it is the hall of the same name where aspiring musicians give recitals and sometimes assure their fame overnight) and then turn left at Hinde Street where there is a massive and gloomy-looking Methodist church with a jolly spire. It also stages concerts given by students of the Trinity College of Music in Mandeville Place; some of them may well be heard later at the Wigmore Hall. Cross Mandeville Place and go on into Manchester Square where, on the north side, you will find the Wallace Collection. And that is why we have come here, to this part of London which I don't much like.

The Wallace Collection has a curious history and is here today largely because of the intransigence of a French woman who married the illegitimate son of the fourth Marquess of Hertford. The Hertford family owned much property in London and, in 1798, purchased the house built for the Duke of Manchester twenty-two years earlier. After his death it became the Spanish embassy for several years until its next owner rechristened it Hertford House. The Hertfords were diplomats who enjoyed Paris where the fourth Marquis, who was unmarried, gave his time almost entirely to collecting. What we see today is part of what he amassed and subsequently bequeathed to his bastard son, Wallace. Because he was born out of wedlock, Wallace could not inherit the marquisate but, during the Franco-Prussian war, and especially whilst Paris was beseiged in 1871, he was responsible for so much charitable work that he was given a Baronetcy. He moved to London with his French wife and about half his collection,

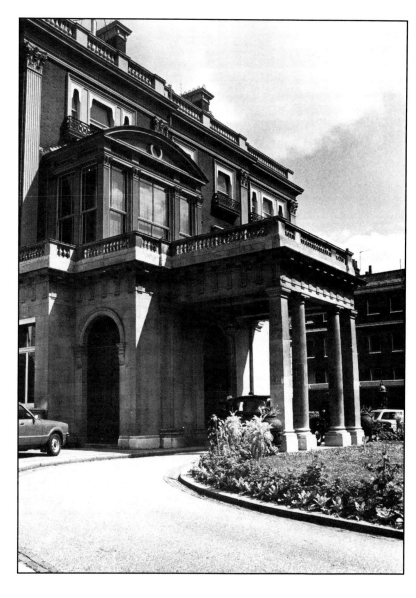

Wallace Collection
Manchester Square

which was eventually left to the nation. Widow Wallace, despite her refusal to speak English, bullied the government into accepting, on behalf of a grateful country, her terms, which were that nothing should be added to or removed from the collection (even on temporary loan); that the Government should purchase a permanent home for it and that it should be called the Wallace Collection. So, ironically, Hertford House was leased and the collection is still there today. It is surely frustrating for the curator to know that it must remain totally unaltered but there is so much to see that it might well

take a lifetime to absorb it all. It is especially rich in eighteenth-century French paintings which are somewhat crowded together in gallery 21. (Note the famous *Gilles and his Family*, by Watteau, and Fragonard's *The Swing*.) There is, however, a wide variety from elsewhere: Canalettos, Guardis, a Rembrandt, Frans Hals's *Laughing Cavalier*, Lawrence's captivating Countess of Blessington and, for me, in gallery 10, the gems of the collection, Richard Bonington's water-colours of Bologna, Venice, Rouen and the Normandy coast. Bonington died aged only 26 but during his short life his genius flamed. For once the great Turner, who also is represented here by water-colours, is outshone. This is also a rewarding museum for those who love French porcelain, furniture, and ormolu clocks, but above all for anyone interested in arms and armour, of which there is so much that I doubt if the curator could ever be entirely certain that the collection had gained a sword or lost one. It was Wallace who added this dimension to his father's collection, much of which was abandoned in Paris and subsequently sold. The house is open all weekdays 10–5, Sundays 2–5, but closed on bank holidays. Admission is free.

Leave Manchester Square by Fitzhardinge Street. Fitzhardinge, who was related to Berkeley, who became Portman, and spawned squares, did not get one named after him, only a street, which leads into Portman Square where we turn left, approaching Oxford Street again. As we near it, on our left, is the gigantic edifice occupying an entire block, the department store named after Gordon Selfridge, an American millionaire who became a naturalized Briton in 1937. He had a vision of creating the grandest, most beautiful department store ever. It took twenty years to complete and it is certainly very imposing, with massive columns rising from the first floor to the fourth, forming a frame around the steel interior. It is the largest of the many stores lining Oxford Street and now has an hotel attached to it. It lacks the grandeur of Harrods (although it is not smothered in fairy lights) and the chic of Liberty's, but for thousands, perhaps millions, it is *the* place to shop, and it draws the campers-out immediately after Christmas when the queues form, almost before the turkeys are cold, for the biggest of the annual sales. To end the Christmas holiday thus, in a sleeping-bag on a pavement, smacks of wilful masochism.

Cross abominable Oxford Street once again, noting the few rogue private drivers who dare to go about their own business on four wheels in a thoroughfare now designated for Buses and Taxis Only. North Audley Street leads us into Grosvenor Square, the largest in Mayfair, and now, for most practical purposes, Little America. The

Mayfair public library
South Audley Street
(opposite)

first US Minister to Britain, in 1789, lived at No. 9, about sixty years after the square had been laid out. The present United States embassy, occupying the entire western side is, according to David Piper, 'under its brooding eagle . . . an admirable expression of almost Roman power'. Well, some of us are democrats, and some republicans. To me the building conveys America's paranoid fear of Europe and the New World. It stands behind a ramp symbolic of a tank trap, and quite useless as defence against the nuclear attack which US policy seems determined to provoke. Perhaps it is deliberate protection against civil disturbance? No doubt the diplomats who work within grow frantic each day as they see ordinary British citizens parking their cars around the square on meters. To them, each and every one feeding in their coins must seem a superspy. Forget them, and admire the statue of that wise man, Franklin Delano Roosevelt. Inside the square, tranquillized against the traffic, he stands leaning on a stick, and is not depicted confined to his wheelchair with a rug across his paralysed legs. The statue was unveiled by his widow, Eleanor, in 1948.

The American link continues in South Audley Street by which we leave. Down on the left is the Grosvenor Chapel which faces Hyde Park at the end of Aldford Street. Without its spire it could easily be taken for a theatre with four widely-spaced pillars holding up the portico. It almost resembles a toy building with its simple tower placed dead centre against, not above, an equally basic pediment. On either side are two Norman windows. It was built in 1730 as a private place of worship for those living on the Grosvenor Estate, and became a chapel of ease for St George's, Hanover Square, a century later. During World War Two American servicemen made it 'their' parish church.

Going down South Audley Street and looking along the prosperous side roads you may well imagine yourself in Forsyte territory. This has always been an affluent quarter of London and still is, although today many of the once elegant drawing-rooms are filled with desks and filing-cabinets. The chandeliers may well have been replaced by strip lighting and Anglepoise lamps, but the pile of the carpet in the executive suites is probably deeper than in more gracious times.

At Curzon Street turn left and note the cool refinement of Crewe House, an eighteenth-century mansion lying back behind railings and a lawn. It confers distinction and was here before the surrounding streets were built. *It* is not in the wrong environment, although it might indeed look more in place in the Surrey hills: *they* are. It is now the headquarters of a trading group, but has been offered for sale. Beyond it, cross to an opening taking you into Shepherd Market, but

Crewe House
Curzon Street

before doing so you may wish to visit Heywood Hill's along on the left. It has a Queen Anne bow window and, some would say, as much right as Hatchard's to be thought of as London's most fashionable bookshop, just as the cinema named Curzon has to rank amongst the élite of the capital's picture-houses. Near the latter is the way into the market called after Edward Shepherd who established it, having leased land from Lord Curzon. Shepherd also laid out many streets in this part of Mayfair.

If it is time for lunch, there is a pub called the Bunch of Grapes where you can struggle through the throng to reach the staircase to a serve-yourself restaurant on the first floor. It has a wide range of hot and cold dishes, and the house wine is good. You may be lucky and find an empty table by a window overlooking the small market area. There are shops down there selling useful ironmongery and other everyday objects, perishable and lasting, as well as antiques all of fifty years old. Shepherd Market is not especially fascinating for what it has to sell but holds its own, balancing carefully on a fence somewhere

between ostentation and quiet expertise. Leave it by the southern exit furthest away from the Grapes – no compass required – and return to Piccadilly, one side of which is here Green Park. On Sundays there will be artists displaying their work against the railings, and making sales, all of them deservedly, if what they have created finds a loving wall space. You can take a rest in the park but it is better to leave that until after a visit to the Wellington Museum in Apsley House which stands on an island or two at Hyde Park Corner. Everything here is broken up by roads and underpasses. Over to your left at the top of Constitution Hill is a great Corinthian archway with a chariot on top driven by four colossal horses. The designer, an army officer who was also a vet, held a dinner for eight inside one of the nags before the statue was completed. Originally the Duke of Wellington stood on this arch, at the entrance to the hill on which no less than three attempts were made on the life of Queen Victoria. It was no criticism of him that he was carried off to Aldershot. He was not trigger happy: it was just that fashions changed and he found himself, on another statue, in front of Apsley House, which is next to a triumphal screen also placed there in his honour.

The Wellington Museum is now administered by the V&A and is open to the public on weekdays 10–6, Sundays 2.30–6. It is worth a visit, but make sure you use the pedestrian underpass to reach its rather uninviting frontage. Within is the room where the Iron Duke held annual banquets on the anniversary of Waterloo. There is a long, wide, highly-polished table with a centrepiece of gleaming silver. In a room beside it are cabinets of plate and china, and in the largest chamber on the same floor is the Waterloo Gallery. In it are hung a great many pictures acquired during the Peninsular Wars, after the first of which Wellington was actually accused of having let off the French too lightly. So he went back and pushed them over the Pyrenees, perhaps acquiring more of these pictures on the way. It is now high time that someone cleaned them.

In the well of a lovely staircase is a fearsome statue of the naked Napoleon, by Canova. In the basement the narrow corridors are lined with such trophies as the battle order for Waterloo and the procession order for the Duke's funeral which provoked a memorable outbreak of the national genius for pageantry. There are also framed cartoons relating to Wellington's life and deeds, as soldier and as politician. His portrait, by Lawrence, is hung in the attractive striped drawing-room on the first floor. (A contemporary Wellington still has private apartments in the house.)

After traipsing about so many streets and squares a walk in Hyde Park will make a pleasing change, and give Park Lane, viewed across

Mayfair
Charles Street
(opposite)

The Wellington Arch
Hyde Park Corner

belts of green and roadway, an extra layer of romance. Hyde Park was once monastic land: later it was used as a forest for hunting by Henry VIII. It has been a royal park ever since, except during the brief Commonwealth at the start of which the Roundheads (the Baddies if you were a royalist) fortified it against threats from the Cavaliers (the Goodies if you weren't a puritan). It covers 361 acres and is one of the two largest lungs of inner London (Regent's Park is the other). There are carriage drives where society once rode on horseback to see and be seen; roads, paths and walks. A few mostly lodge-type buildings are dotted about it but there is also a substantial police station. Prince Albert's 1851 Exhibition was held here and since then it has been the venue for great rallies of one sort or another, some peaceful, others seething with militancy against some aspects of government policy. Primarily, however, it has been a playground for Londoners, a vast area of green laid out informally, for the most part, for their delight. It is cut off now, from the east, by the broad multi-carriage ways enabling the traffic to speed from one end of Park Lane to the other, and to reach the next traffic jam that much more quickly. The Lane, as it is not very happily named for its present function, has many hotels – the Dorchester, Grosvenor House and the Hilton amongst them. At the northern end terraces of houses which surprise by their almost total lack of uniformity still remain. Their appearance suggests that they have been inherited, in equal part, by the many eccentric sons of one dynasty, and that those offspring have been determined to imprint on each bequest their own personalities. In fact, these are the backs of the original Georgian houses whose gardens bordered the lane between the properties and the park. And they are more beautiful than the fronts of most houses.

Beneath the ground on which we are now walking is a car-park to take one thousand vehicles. It has a main entrance near Speakers' Corner, the tarmacked area at the north-east of the square where the British tradition of free speech is upheld every Sunday for certain, but also at other times, when those with religious, political or social messages come here to harangue the passers-by. Many stop to listen and thus contribute to what is a most valuable safety-valve in our democratic system. The speakers range from out-and-out cranks to the highly esteemed Donald (now Lord) Soper, the pacifist Methodist minister who has had a regular pitch here for more than half a century. It is essential to an understanding of the English – possibly the British – character to experience a Sunday afternoon at Speakers' Corner. When you have done so, and cast a look in the direction of the Marble Arch, which used to stand in front of Buckingham Palace and is of no great moment except that it is there and has been part of the landscape for a long time, go and relax in the truly king-sized park.

Walk Eight

Trafalgar Square – Suffolk Street – Haymarket –
Royal Opera Arcade – Waterloo Place –
Carlton House Terrace – Lower Regent Street –
Piccadilly Circus – Regent Street – Carnaby Street –
Oxford Circus – Langham Place – Portland Place –
Park Crescent – Regent's Park

*Regent's Canal
passing through
the Zoo*

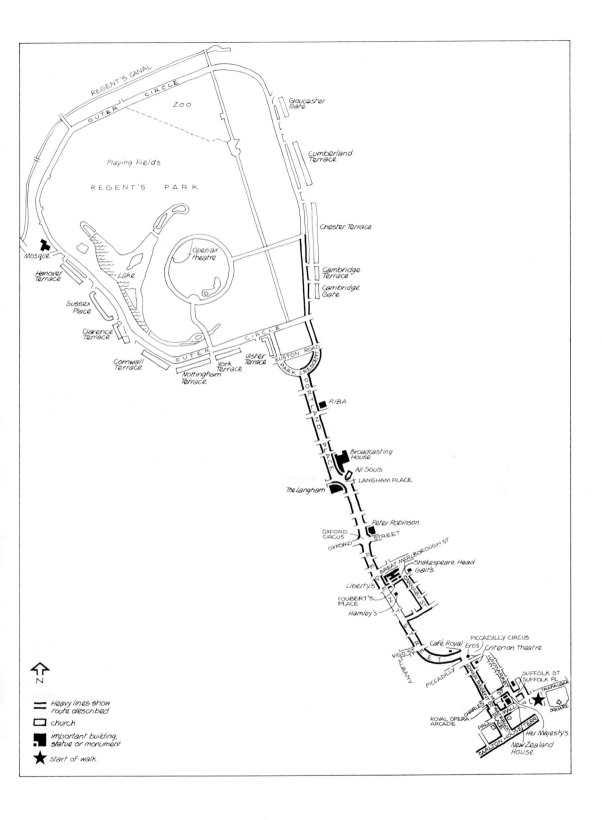

REGENT'S CANAL

OUTER CIRCLE

ZOO

Gloucester Gate

Cumberland Terrace

Playing Fields

REGENT'S PARK

Chester Terrace

Mosque

Open air theatre

Cambridge Terrace

Cambridge Gate

Hanover Terrace

Lake

Sussex Place

Clarence Terrace

OUTER CIRCLE

Ulster Terrace

EUSTON ROAD

PARK CRESCENT

RIBA

Cornwall Terrace

York Terrace

Nottingham Terrace

PORTLAND PLACE

Broadcasting House

All Souls

LANGHAM PLACE

The Langham

Peter Robinson

OXFORD CIRCUS

OXFORD STREET

GREAT MARLBOROUGH ST

Shakespeare Head

Galt's

Liberty's

FOUBERT'S PLACE

Hamley's

Café Royal

Eros

PICCADILLY CIRCUS

Criterion Theatre

VIGO ST

ALBANY

PICCADILLY

SUFFOLK ST

SUFFOLK PL

TRAFALGAR SQUARE

ROYAL OPERA ARCADE

HAYMARKET

PALL MALL

CHARLES II

Her Majesty's

CARLTON HOUSE TERR

New Zealand House

N

Heavy lines show route described

church

important building, statue or monument

start of walk

This last walk from Trafalgar Square, once under way, follows broadly the route of John Nash's grand scheme for connecting St James's Park with Regent's Park, his so-called Via Triumphalis. As you follow it you may feel the same sadness which I experience, that it was not entirely realized, and that so little of what was, has survived.

We will enter by the side door as it were, up Suffolk Street and into Suffolk Place, both now heavily overlooked by New Zealand House. (Leave the square by its north-west corner along Pall Mall East and turn right.) The Suffolks were supportive features in the design, adding a necessary peripheral touch. Now they are almost all that remains at this end. The Place comes out into Haymarket opposite Her Majesty's Theatre (French château style, 1890s) which looks less imposing than once it did because of New Zealand House, 225 feet high with a glass and concrete tower rising to fifteen storeys. On the fourteenth level is the Martini Terrace where publishers and others hold promotional launches, and where Hatchard's Bookshop throws its Authors of the Year party. The view over London is stunning, making one feel airborne, but not just with words.

At ground level turn right to admire London's most elegant playhouse, the Theatre Royal, Haymarket, the front of which is by Nash. It stands behind six columns supporting a portico over the pavement and within there is an auditorium which is sheer delight and in which I have seen and heard plays at all levels for forty years. It is perfect for stylish comedy, for Congreve, Sheridan, Maugham. The Theatre Royal dates back to 1720 when the Haymarket lived up to its name, and stood opposite Sir John Vanbrugh's theatre on the site of Her Majesty's. Hay has not been on sale in the street since about 1830. Today, when you come to it, other than for plays and films, you are likely to be looking for Burberry's to buy a raincoat, or for the American Express office. Cross Haymarket at the lights to Charles II Street where, beyond the side of Her Majesty's, is the delectable Royal Opera Arcade in which Nash also had a hand. It is lined, on its west side, with small bow-fronted shops which have spiral staircases to their low upper floors. Happily the arcade was incorporated into the design for New Zealand House. When you come out of it, cross Pall Mall and go into Waterloo Place, where you can again admire the friezes on the Athenaeum and the Institute of Directors. We saw them in the previous walk but they can be borne twice in a lifetime and after visiting Carlton House Terrace they must be endured again. From all that one hears about Nash's indifference to commonplace problems of building, we should think ourselves lucky that anything of his has survived. He was a man with a grand vision but Wren would probably not have approved of his neglect of certain structural

*Theatre Royal
Haymarket*

principles. This I cannot verify for myself, not being an engineer, but it is what the experts say. He was, apparently, a shoddy workman, and what remains to please our eye is costly to maintain. We must just be grateful that it is here, certainly in the case of Carlton House Terrace which, despite improvements, is a pleasure from both the domesticated frontage which we see on this occasion and from the more impressive aspect facing the Mall. Up here, on Waterloo Place, it is a terrace of houses in which it would be wholly acceptable to live: on the other side, where all the columns are, you might find it difficult to behave naturally if you found yourself on view. Your teeth and lips might form CHEESE automatically, your right hand give a regal wave. Here you could let yourself in with a latchkey and not have too great a risk of being mugged. There are railed-off gardens between the fronts of the terraces and the backs of Pall Mall clubs, and there is a road through from the latter ending in a fairly pleasant-looking office block. Statues and plaques abound, of course. Queen Victoria is under a portico on the east terrace, her son, the first 'teddy boy', is in Waterloo Place, and his grandson, George VI, as we saw in Walk Three, is at the top of a flight of steps down to the Mall. At No. 4 Carlton Gardens, Lord Palmerston, the Tory MP who became a Whig prime minister, although that made little difference to his innately conservative nature, lived from 1846 to 1855. In the Second World War it became General de Gaulle's headquarters from which he rallied the Free French fighting forces and railed intermittently against Churchill and the British government. The plaque to him is in French and has a facsimile of his signature. Across the way, at No. 2, another soldier, Kitchener, lived in 1914–15 in what is now the Royal Fine Arts Commission's home.

This is the London of top people and incomes, yet only a small part of it – where they come to work, sit in committee or confer over lunch. They actually live miles away in Herts and Bucks and Surrey, but you can feel their presence here in quiet enclaves where campaigns have been planned. No doubt I fantasize but that is another pleasure of walking a city, and it puts you in a mood, as you return through Waterloo Place to Lower Regent Street, to see what Nash in his mind saw: a wide carriageway bending gently northwards, first to Piccadilly, then crossing Oxford Street and Euston Road to end in the largest of circuses in Europe at the entrance to the Regent's park. The Regent, later George IV, was his patron, but lost interest before the scheme was completed. Today there is a wide thoroughfare to take us up to Piccadilly Circus and into the Quadrant at the bottom of Regent Street which follows a curve now lined with handsome buildings, by Sir Reginald Blomfield. But there is nothing of Nash's extant.

Piccadilly Circus is for many people quite simply the statue of Eros which stands joyfully in its centre. Eros was the Greek god of love and rather surprisingly in this instance he commemorates the 7th Earl of Shaftesbury, a great Victorian reformer who did much to improve conditions for working women and children in an age when they were unprotected. His statue could have been yet another of an upstanding nobleman surrounded by symbols of his good deeds and clad in classical gear. Classical it is, but Sir Alfred Gilbert settled on Eros and a fountain, and this feature almost alone bestows distinction on the circus. I qualify the statement because the Quadrant follows Nash's plan and also because, on the southern side, is the quite enchanting little Criterion Theatre, constructed like a temple of pagan worship, below street level. Eros might almost be aiming his arrow at this exquisite playhouse out of which you walk, at upper circle level, on to the pavement of Lower Regent Street. It was threatened with

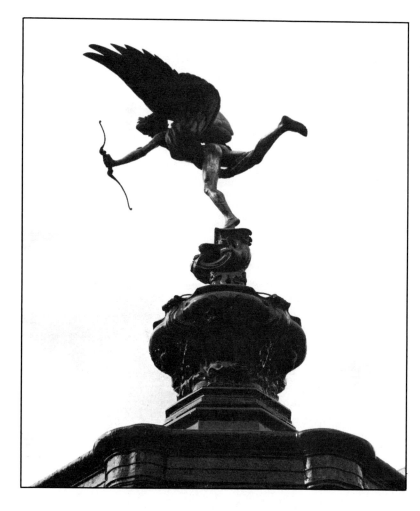

Eros
Piccadilly Circus

demolition along with the restaurant of the same name – now closed
– and other buildings on the south side of the circus (which is no
more round than many squares are square). If the developers win I
hope the theatre may be incorporated in the new design, as happened
to another down at Hammersmith.

Now we go into Regent Street which is dominated by travel
offices, department stores, classy men's outfitters, the best known of
toyshops (Hamleys) and, at the lower end, the Cafe Royal, with suites
of banqueting rooms and memories of *fin-de-siècle* days when Oscar
Wilde and the fashionable literati of his time met and posed there.
Almost opposite is Vigo Street where, to the left of the entrance to
Albany, were the first offices of the Bodley Head, from which John
Lane published the *Yellow Book* with Beardsley's drawings. Lane used
to examine Beardsley's drawings with a powerful magnifying glass in

order to identify and then remove the artist's minute obscenities. Nowadays he would enlarge them.

Regent Street comes into its own at Christmastide when clusters of fairy lights in intricate design are strung across it to attract the shoppers. Some years a royal personage switches them on. In all years they cause Sunday evening traffic jams when Greater Londoners come out in their cars to gape at them. The stores and shops bear formidable names. Behind Liberty's, high on the eastern side, lies Carnaby Street, a relic of the swinging London of the 1960s, now rather *passé* but still in business. It is pedestrianized and the noise comes mostly from the loud pop blaring from the shops. It is bright and cheerful and the pavement is made of colourful rubberized blocks. Much of the early-nineteenth-century, perhaps late-eighteenth-century, building remains above the jazzy shopfronts but there is also a tendency to mock Tudor, most marked in the Shakespeare Head hostelry which has a bust of the bard hanging outside. Here also is Galt's which rivals Hamleys for parents who are into meaningful toys. (Which do the kids prefer?) Mock Tudory occurs again as we leave to return to Regent Street, down Foubert's Place and across a road which seems to belong to Liberty's who certainly have a covered passage across at a higher level to take clients from their Elizabethan emporium into their Regent Street palace. The latter faces the world stonily and has a frieze in the centre of which is a figure looking like Britannia. There is much movement to left and right of her and someone seems to be approaching with a gun carriage. From the parapet above three godly figures observe the scene unmoved. The other Liberty's, down Great Marlborough Street, is really imitation Tudor carried to a point of absurdity. There are twisted chimneys, one of which has a golden galleon on it, and the windows which should be letting light into the store are finicky little leaded panels. Yet Liberty's, once heavily committed to Art Nouveau which, in Italian, is *stile Liberty*, survives and to some, no doubt, its frontage and interior are symbols of lasting values.

Continue up Regent Street to Oxford Circus where another famous store, Peter Robinson, faces you, but soon your eye will travel to an altogether more engaging sight – Nash's church of All Souls, Langham Place, a novel design with the tower in a circular surround of pillars and a spire above a colonnaded round platform. The whole is built to one side of the long rectangle in which there is both church and hall. The site was a swamp so Nash had to lay his foundations very deep, which served the church well when, in the mid 1970s, there was urgent need for a hall. So the floor of the nave was lifted by 18 inches and the Waldegrave Room made beneath it. It is the only

Arts and Crafts decoration Harley Street, parallel to Portland Place (opposite)

*Broadcasting
House*

remaining Nash church in London, it is 'high' in Church of England terminology and the singing of the choir is much recorded. Amongst the pillars at lower level is a statue of Nash.

Originally the church pointed the way rather cleverly to Portland Place, just as the Quadrant buildings led the eye from Lower Regent Street obliquely across Piccadilly Circus to Regent Street itself. But

Broadcasting House (1931) has rather spoiled Nash's ingenious plan and heaves heavily down upon his church, which also suffers competition from the former Langham Hotel, now an annexe of the BBC. Broadcasting House is, appropriately, built of Portland stone and looks rather like a ship of state ready to float gently down

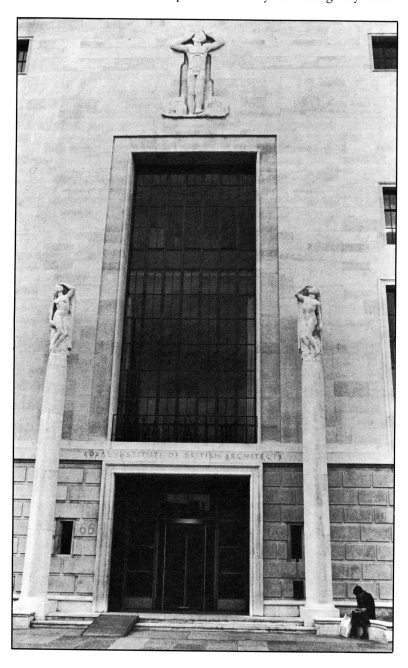

Royal Institute of British Architects Portland Place

towards St James's. It has sculptures by Eric Gill. Old Father Time, or maybe *his* father, is holding a young person as they both balance on a globe. This is the headquarters of BBC sound; television is out at Shepherd's Bush and beyond the scope of this book; the world service we have already met at Aldwych. From time to time governments look askance at the BBC, as do those commercial moguls who resent its independence and monopoly of licence fees. To me, for all its extravagance, bureaucracy and arrogance, the Beeb, or 'Aunty' as it is affectionately, perhaps a little derisively, called, is a good deed in a naughty world. What other country can boast a broadcasting system untethered to the political party in power and standing aloof from the profit motive? It is Speakers' Corner updated. We should cherish it.

The road curves round to Portland Place, the proportions of which are the same as when Nash envisaged the Adam terraces there as part of his grand design. Those terraces have suffered from bombing, rebuilding and redesign; the exceptionally wide street (110 feet) has been divided not only to provide a space for statuary but also for metered parking-places, so the broad aspect upon which Foley House (now the Langham Hotel) once looked out has been diminished. This in the street where the RIBA (Royal Institute of British Architects) has its headquarters. Never mind, it could be a marvellous mall again (though that is unlikely) along which traffic, stately and otherwise, might sweep to the most magnificent part of Nashville, the apotheosis of our walk – Park Crescent and the Outer Circle of Regent's Park itself, dominated still by the terraces with which the great architect bordered it.

The Crescent was supposed to have been a circus which would have had a larger diameter than any in Europe. It was only half completed but it is superb – two quarter crescents which, at pavement level, are colonnaded along their entire exquisitely curving lengths. Above are sweeps of balcony with first-floor windows arched, except near the ends. It is one of the most impressive sights in London, as are the terraces on the Outer Circle with their painted pediments and classical statues. The exteriors have been preserved, at great cost, around most of Regent's Park; inside the shortcomings of Nash as builder have caused them to be gutted and restyled for present-day practical use. I do not at all mind that these buildings are whited sepulchres – I saw some of the façades being upheld whilst their interiors were being totally reconstructed. Nash's Via Triumphalis was a theatrical conception. What we now see surrounding the Park are the act drops against which the modern city plays, and it is fortunate that the architect's further plans to build inside the wide green space were not allowed, for financial considerations, to come to

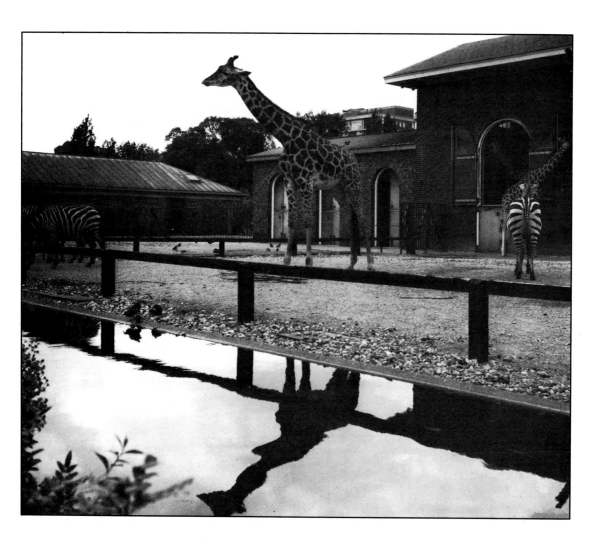

fruition. London needs Regent's Park as a vital lung and it has it, *Giraffes and Zebras* complete with Zoo, Open Air Theatre, lake, playing fields, canal and *at the London Zoo* even a mosque.

*   *   *   *

We have seen, in these walks, three cathedrals, an abbey, dozens of churches, many museums and galleries, statues and busts galore, department stores, shops, clubs, markets, theatres. We have been into tranquil squares and parks, noted terraces of handsome houses, crossed bridges real and metaphorical, considered the character of one area and compared it with another. We have trudged along almost all of the most famous streets and a great many of the minor ones as well, yet still we have seen only a fraction of what is London, that 'unique city' as the Danish commentator Steen Eiler Rasmussen called it. He used it for the title of the book he wrote in 1934, one of the most perceptive ever written about the capital, and to describe what he called the 'scattered city', one that has grown outwards, not upwards like most. This is no longer as true as when Rasmussen was first published but it does account for many famous aspects of London not being mentioned in my book. I believe London to be too scattered, but that is the price we have paid for being 'unique' in the Dane's reckoning, of insisting on living in little villas, each with our own garden, and on having so many parks and green squares in the inner city. In ancient Rome the sports stadium, called the Colosseum, stood in its centre. In London the permanent homes of sport are at Wembley, Wimbledon, St John's Wood. The overflow of the British Museum is out in Middlesex; London University has satellites in Hampstead and down in Surrey. The Botanical Gardens are miles away in Kew; the television centre is in Shepherd's Bush; the nearest cemetery to the centre is at Kensal Green; the closest pleasure gardens at Battersea.

We have seen much on these walks, yet only scratched the surface. But, as J. G. Links might say, there is another day, and another visit. Relax now and savour what you have seen.

Bibliography

There are literally thousands of publications on London, from pamphlets to works in many volumes. This is a select list of those I found most helpful in writing this book.

Banks, F. R., *The Penguin Guide To London*, 1977.

Barker, Felix and Hyde, Ralph, *London: 2000 Years Of A City And Its People*, Cassell, 1974.

London As It Might Have Been, Murray, 1982.

Blatch, Mervyn, *A Guide To London Churches*, Constable, 1978.

Byron, Arthur, *London Statues*, Constable, 1981.

City of London, The, *Official Guide*, n.d.

Clunn, Harold, *The Face Of London*, Spring Books, n.d.

Dakers, Caroline, *The Blue Plaque Guide To London*, Macmillan, 1981.

Ekwall, Eilert, *Street Names Of The City Of London*, Clarendon Press, 1954.

Fairfield, S., *The Streets Of London*, Macmillan, 1983.

Ferris, Paul, *The City*, Gollancz, 1960.

Field, John, *Place-Names Of Greater London*, Batsford, 1980.

Jones, Edward and Woodward, Christopher, *A Guide To The Architecture Of London*, Weidenfeld & Nicolson, 1983.

Kent, William, *An Encyclopaedia Of London*, Dent, 1951.

Pevsner, Nikolaus, *The Buildings Of England: London Volume One: The Cities of London and Westminster*, Third Edition revised by Bridget Cherry, Penguin, 1973.

London Except the Cities of London and Westminster, Penguin, 1952.

Piper, David, *London, An Illustrated Companion Guide*, Collins, 1980.

Pritchett, V. S., *London Perceived*, Heinemann/Chatto & Windus, 1962.

Rasmussen, Steen Eiler, *London: The Unique City*, Penguin, 1960.

Rogers, Malcolm, *Blue Guide To The Museums And Galleries Of London*, Benn, 1983.

Service, Alastair, *The Architects Of London*, Architectural Press, 1979.

Stow, John, *Survey Of London 1598*, Dent, 1912.

Also the official guides to the British Museum, the National Gallery, the National Portrait Gallery, the Museum of London, and to numerous palaces, churches, houses, galleries, museums, etc., mentioned in the text.

Index

Page numbers in bold type indicate main entry. Numbers in italic refer to illustrations. (The following subjects are listed in groups – Churches; City Livery Companies and Halls; Kings and Queens; Public Houses; Theatres.)